~~YOU SAID ONE THING...~~

GOD SAID DIFFERENTLY

Silencing the Unauthorized Voices and Living your Authentic Life

Copyright © 2018 by Jonathan Wesley

Published by AuthorsUnite.com

TABLE OF
CONTENTS

Dedication

Prologue

About the Author

DEDICATION

This book is dedicated to the late Theresa M. Wesley who was my mother. She passed two days before my birthday and she was my main supporter. She loved me being her son, walking in truth, love, prayer, authenticity and in ministry. She raised me as a single parent and she did a great job if I can say so myself. This book is in her honor specifically, as well as in the honor of all persons that I have had the pleasure of mentoring and serving throughout the years. Your lives and your resilience caused me to place the ink to the paper and write. My prayer is that this book challenges you to live in truth and share your story so that the lives of others can be impacted positively, and God gets the glory out of it all. All that I have sought to do and accomplish in life has been to make God and my mother proud of me. My journey has been authentic and a struggle. However, the reward is knowing that they both are smiling down on me and are guiding me through this journey called life. Thank you all for your continued support and my hope is that you are blessed by this book. Read it with an open heart and open spirit in order to receive the true message which will be found in the pages following this dedication.

Romans 8:28 reads "And we know that all things work together for the good of them who love the Lord. Those who have been called according to his purpose" (KJV).

Yours in His Service,

Jonathan Wesley, M.Ed., Certified Pastoral Counselor*The Motivator, The Enthusiast, The Professor, The Counselor*

PROLOGUE

In the book of the Prophet Jeremiah, Chapter 1 verses 5-19 says; *"Then the word of the LORD came unto me, saying, Before I formed thee in the belly I knew thee; and before thou camest forth out of the womb I sanctified thee, and I ordained thee a prophet unto the nations. Then said I, Ah, Lord GOD! Behold, I cannot speak: for I am a child. But the LORD said unto me, Say not, I am a child: for thou shalt go to all that I shall send thee, and whatsoever I command thee thou shalt speak. Be not afraid of their faces: for I am with thee to deliver thee, saith the LORD. Then the LORD put forth his hand, and touched my mouth. And the LORD said unto me, Behold, I have put my words in thy mouth. See, I have this day set thee over the nations and over the kingdoms, to root out, and to pull down, and to destroy, and to throw down, to build, and to plant. Thou therefore gird up thy loins, and arise, and speak unto them all that I command thee: be not dismayed at their faces, lest I confound thee before them. For, behold, I have made thee this day a defensed city, and an iron pillar, and brazen walls against the whole land, against the kings of Judah, against the princes thereof, against the priests thereof, and against the people of the land. And they shall fight against thee; but they shall not prevail against thee; for I am with thee, saith the LORD, to deliver thee."*

The word that I, The Lord, spoke to Jeremiah many centuries ago is the same call that applies to those special ones that I have called in this 21st century. The thing about me is that my ways are not the ways of man, nor are my thoughts. I possess infinite wisdom and I use the foolish things to confound the wise. Many will never understand my ways. Many do not believe in me even though I grace them with life every day. See, having a calling and an assignment is not always easy. Trust me! I know firsthand. I had to come down from my throne to save the world! Who really wants to be born into a sinful nature and travel through life being misunderstood? That is not an ideal life for anyone; however, it was chosen for me. I worked hard being a carpenter, but also doing the work of my father. I started doing ministry at age 30 and my assignment was over at age 33. I traveled the land, healed people, spoke wisdom, cast out devils, fed the multitudes, and restored the earth. Even while I was doing these works, those who preached about my arrival did not even recognize me. How can you preach about someone for centuries and not recognize me, even when the proof is evident? It is amazing how quickly people can turn on others, and it is challenging when life becomes so isolating. I had twelve disciples around me, yet some of them did not even know me in the power of my might. Some denied me and one betrayed me to the point of my crucifixion.

The agony of carrying a cross while being beaten was just horrible. I even asked myself if this cup would pass, but I understood that it was the will of my Father to accomplish what had to be done, for I was the only one anointed to do it. After being crucified and giving up the ghost, I had to go to hell, set captivity captive, and ascend back to my throne. I sent to the world a comforter, in the form of the Holy Spirit. Whoever believes in me shall have everlasting life. I did all that I was instructed to do so that you today, reading this book, can understand that life is worth living.

As indicated in Jeremiah, I have called and will call many people. Even with their flaws, age, and disposition. My will still must be fulfilled in the earth. All I need is a willing vessel. The call that I have made on my people was ordained before they were even born into the earth. The challenge is accepting the call and doing what I have instructed. The calling is not always glamorous and it is very costly. If a person were really a believer, then they would know that already based upon my own life. I had to forsake a lot in order to fulfill my assignment, but not everyone is willing to take on the same task. There was one that I anointed, and validated to do great things in the earth. His name is Terrell Adams. I placed on him, such a strong call, that he did not understand. I enjoy the fact that he remained faithful to me despite the trials and tribulations that he would endure. This is a story of how his life and struggles were used to bring me glory. I would encourage you to pay attention to his life and example. Not all words from me will come across a pulpit. Know the words that you are reading are designed to change your life and method of thinking forever.

CHAPTER 1
The Initial Call

"Praise the Lord Everyone. We have gathered into this place to magnify the name of the Lord and give him the praise that he is due. It is an honor to stand before you today to proclaim the good news of Jesus Christ. If you would take this journey with me in your Bible, turn to Luke 15:15-24 and then verses 31-32. The scripture reads as followed: *And he went and joined himself to a citizen of that country; and he sent him into his fields to feed swine. And he would fain have filled his belly with the husks that the swine did eat: and no man gave unto him. And when he came to himself, he said, How many hired servants of my father's have bread enough and to spare, and I perish with hunger! I will arise and go to my father, and will say unto him, Father, I have sinned against heaven, and before thee And am no more worthy to be called thy son: make me as one of thy hired servants. And he arose, and came to his father. But when he was yet a great way off, his father saw him, had compassion, ran, fell on his neck, and kissed him. And the son said unto him, Father, I have sinned against heaven, and in thy sight, and am no more worthy to be called thy son. But the father said to his servants, Bring forth the best robe, and put it on him; and put a ring on his hand, and shoes on his feet: And bring hither the fatted calf, and kill it; and let us eat, and be merry: For this my son was dead, and is alive again; he was lost, and is found. And they began to be merry."* Verses 31-32 read *"And he said unto him, Son, thou art ever with me, and all that I have is thine. It was meet that we should make merry, and be glad: for this thy brother was dead, and is alive again; and was lost, and is found."*

RETURN! I AM WAITING

"The topic for today is 'Return! I am waiting.' In the text here, we have the story of the prodigal son. We have the father who is the head of the house and two sons who are nameless. In the text, the older son is deemed as being the perfect child. He was content with living at home with his father and he did not want for anything. The family was wealthy and he was fine just being in the house. On the other hand, we have the youngest son, the ambitious one. The one that believed that he had experienced enough in his father's house and figured that it was time to move on. Many times, we as people move before our time. We may feel the inclination to move forward and take what belongs to us, however, if we are not careful, we have the ability to squander, that which belongs to us.

"Here we have the youngest son that tells his dad that he wants his portion of his inheritance. The father did not argue with his son, but he allowed him to have what rightfully belonged to him. The son took all that he had and journeyed to a country that was far, and wasted what belonged to him. He did not waste his goods on things that would benefit him, but the scripture tells us that he spent it on riotous living. In other words, he was celebrating. Living the dream life and doing anything that seemed right in his eyes. As soon as he spent all that he had, there arose a mighty famine in the land and the son became desperate. He was in need. He wanted now, what he had just wasted. It is just like the enemy to trick us into thinking that what we have will last forever. The seasoned people had a saying to "get all you can, and can all you get." This statement meant that a person would work and get all that they could while there was a harvest because, in time, a famine would come. When the famine came, if you properly stored away during the harvest, you would be able to survive the famine.

"The son, however, could not survive the famine because he had wasted everything that belonged to him. His life as he knew it was over and at this point the son began to sink. This resembles many of us who have done negative things and caused us to fall into the quicksand of life. The son then joined a country that he was not familiar with, because he did not have the means to return home. Pride was also a major factor. Thus, the son who once lived in the palace is now living in an unknown country with new rules and regulations. Because he spent all that he had, he now had to work in order to survive. He was so broken that he had to feed the swine (pigs).

"Back during that time, if a person even touched a pig, it was viewed as being a disgrace. While feeding the swine and not having any food, the son began to eat the husks that the swine ate. Sometimes when people are in their lowest state, they begin to do things that are not common to them in order to survive. Now, I am sure that as people were passing by, they were looking at him with disgust and mocking him because of his lowly state. The son, however, had no one to blame but himself. He made a conscious decision to spend all that he had, without thinking about the consequences of his actions. Even in all of this, an awakening happened for the youngest son.

"The scripture says in verse 17 that the youngest son came to himself. In life, it takes getting to our lowest point, and being in isolation, for us to come to ourselves. Have you ever been in a horrible situation and wondered how in the world you had arrived to that place? The great thing is that even though he was not in the house of his father, he remembered where he came from. He then began to say to himself that in his father's house, there were hired servants who brought him food. He remembered that in his father's house, there was more than enough food while he was in this foreign country starving. The son then made a decision.

"It is one thing to acknowledge your current situation, but it takes faith to move beyond what you have acknowledged in order to be in a better state of mind. The son made a decision to go back home from whence he came. He acknowledged his wrongdoing. He was so desperate to be back in the comfort of his home that he even decided that he would accept being a servant, and not acknowledged as a son because of how he had disgraced his family.

"One thing about being at a very low point in life is that it should make you humble. If people can really be honest with themselves, they would not return to a place the same way that they left. The son got up from the swine pit and headed to his father's house. Mind you, he did not wash and smelled wretched. Despite what he looked like, he was willing to go back to his father's house. According to verse 20, while he was far off, the father saw him and had compassion. The problem with some church people at times is that if a person like the prodigal son came into a church, the majority of the people would look with a turned up nose and stand in judgment. This is why we must be glad that God is not like man. We must be more like our father who has been, and is waiting on us, to make a conscious choice to return to him as the son did in this story.

"When the son expressed his feelings and confessed his wrongdoings with a spirit of repentance, the father without any questions asked, celebrated his son's return. See, the problem with people is that when a person returns from being away, there is an interrogation session. Sometimes it is not as important to know the backstory. Just celebrate that the person returned alive. If it had not been for the grace of God, we all would have been consumed by the sins we committed when we left his presence.

"According to verses 22-24, the father threw his son a huge party

4

upon his return home. His garments were changed and the son no longer resembled his prodigal experience. He went from being filthy and smelling of swine to being cleansed. He now had clothes to wear, shoes on his feet and instead of eating from the pigpen, he was eating from his father's table. The father was excited because his son, that was dead in his own ways of life, was alive again with a different spirit. He had been lost in a foreign country with foreign rules, but he was now found. The father ran to meet his son from afar and gave him a warm welcome. This is what we must do when our wayward brothers and sisters return home.

"When lost souls come into the house, we must receive them with authentic love and compassion, as Christ received us. However, we find there is always one who will not be excited. Let us take the time to look at the older son who remained in the house. He was thoroughly upset with the fact that his father threw a party to celebrate his younger brother's return. The older brother was jealous because the father had never thrown a party for him though he never left his father's side. We must be mindful of those who are not excited about the restoration of others. The oldest son always had access to the fatted calf, clothes and the necessities of life because he remained in the house where it all was already provided. The father affirmed the son in verse 31, letting him know that he had access to what was being presented to the younger brother. He also let the oldest son know that this is a time to be merry for what was lost is now found. What had died is now alive again and for that, a celebration is in order.

"When we look at the topic of the message for today "Return! I am waiting," we must put our lives in the place of the prodigal son. We all have made some terrible mistakes and some of you that are sitting here in the congregation are still making bad choices. You feel as though you have worked hard to get to where you are and that you do not owe anyone anything. For some of you, even in all that you have or have not accomplished, you know that there is a part of you that is yearning for something more. You are in the pigpen of life when God wants more for you and from you. The great thing about God is that even in your lowly state, he is still with you. The scripture tells us in Matthew 28:20 *"Teaching them to observe all things whatsoever I have commanded you: and, lo, I am with you always, even unto the ends of the world. Amen."*

"Today, God wants you to return to him so that he can give you rest. It does not matter what life you have lived, or how bad the stench of where you are in life smells. Jesus welcomes you back with open arms and with compassion. The angels in heaven are rejoicing that today, you have chosen not to be a prodigal anymore. Not only is God waiting on you, so is your destiny, and those who are connected to it. Think about it, if you decide to stay where you are in life, imagine how many people will never move forward in life. Tomorrow is not promised and I encourage you, my brothers and sisters, to come back to God. He misses spending time with you and he wants your relationship to go to the next level. Once you come back home, you will be empowered through the Holy Spirit to bring others who have been in the same pigpen, back to the father. The father who is loving, caring, compassionate, allpowerful, all knowing and altogether lovely. God is wonderful and he loves you just the way that you are. Allow him to help you be better. As the pastor of this ministry, we will do all that we can to ensure that you have the tools needed to stay on the right path.

"You might be saying to yourself, "Pastor, God does not want me. I have too many issues and I have been hurt so much. God doesn't want anyone like me." I would like to take a moment to challenge your spirit. God does want you. I know because he wanted me. I have many times during my life taken the prodigal route because I did not want to submit to what God had for me. I thought that living life, as a "normal" person would be better; however, I learned the hard way that there is no escape when God is trying to get your attention. Even though people counted me out while I was in the pigpen of life, God counted me in. People that knew me passed me by in the pigpen. Some did not even offer their hand to help, but I know God to be a keeper and a deliverer for myself. When you were down and out, friends left you all alone. God said that you would be as a tree planted by the rivers of water that shall not be moved. It does not matter what they have said. All that matters is what God has said. Your perception about yourself must change today.

"Your obedience to his call for your life will produce glory that he deserves to receive. People do not have a heaven or a hell to put you into unless you allow them to. Greater is He that is in you than he that is in the world. Yes, the words of people hurt and many of you do not want to deal with what people will say, but there is life after the hurt. After the pain, after the agony, after the frustration, after the betrayal, there is still life for you, my brothers and sisters. Know that it does not matter if they said you would not make it in life. God has said something different, and that is all that matters. Therefore, I beseech you brothers and sisters to return to God. He is waiting on your return.

This concludes this Sunday's sermon.

Tell your neighbors, friends and family next time that just because they said you would not make it, God's voice is stronger than that of the naysayer. While the altar is open, I admonish you to come. We will pray with you and offer you Jesus. Come one! Come all! God is waiting on your recommitment."

Now standing in front of a great congregation, I am proud of Terrell as I see him minister my Gospel. I have watched him since he was conceived in the womb of Terrie. Prior to his inception, I had already ordained him to do great things in my name. I am so pleased with how he has turned out. I would say that I am surprised, but I am not. Simply because I created him. Terrell has been through so much in his life. Some had faith in him, and others said that he would not amount to anything simply because of how different he has always been. As we travel back in time, you shall know the importance of Terrell's message.

From the time that he was born to Terrie Adams and James Turner in September 1989, Terrell was always a peculiar child. Even though I allowed him to be born in the rough streets of Newark, NJ to a family that was not educated, I anointed him to be different so that he could lead the way for others. I want Terrell to lead those behind him, as well as those who are older, that desire life in a different manner. Even though his family did not have the best education, one thing that this lineage had, from his grandmother Lilly Adams on down, was a genuine love for me. Lilly instilled my ways into her children and took a special liking to Terrell once he was born. He was always smarter than the others were and he had such an old spirit. His wisdom always exceeded his age and he possessed a love for me that was wonderful even as a child. He was talking before his time and walked early growing up in his single parent home. Along with his mother, Terrie, he had two older sisters that I blessed him with named Latrice and Gabriel Adams. I also blessed him with two other siblings that were his father's children. Terrell has one brother by the name of Tyrell Turner and another sister, Sophia Turner.

His great grandmother Jeter Mae Dixon spoke prophetically the word that I had given her to speak to his mother before he was born which was that he would be a great man in the earth and a prophet. She was right! She was only speaking what I had told her to speak and my word is true and will never return unto me void. The office of the prophet is one that I have bestowed upon this family from generations past. Many of them did not accept the call due to the lack of education. When one person declines, another will accept. Terrell was always a busy body and always talked. As a child, he had a foul mouth. Even though he loved me dearly, he would use profanity in the same sentence. He learned that from his grandmother Lilly. When he was 2 years old, he had a near death experience by sticking scissors into an outlet, but I spared his life! Children will be children, but I had this one covered. He did not suffer any life threatening damage. He was always a very curious child and into everything. He could recite Psalms 23 and constantly prayed at a young age. He loved his Grandma Lilly and Great Grandmother Jeter Mae, and spent plenty of time with them both growing up, until the age of seven when I took Jeter Mae away.

This was a very tragic situation for Terrell because of how close he was to his great grandmother. The funeral was very emotional and Terrell cried the entire time, but little did he know he would see his grandmother again. As the youngest of four, Terrell was very strong emotionally as a child. Despite this fact, there was much in store for him that he did not expect. The great thing about his life is that even through the trials, I sent him reminders that life is worth living.

CHAPTER 2
Danger of Innocence

My son Terrell was the perfect child, so people thought. He was very intelligent, charismatic and very curious. He surely talked the majority of the time as a child, which was a skill he learned from his mother. Along with his intelligence and desire to be in my house the majority of the time, Terrell was always different, and even though he loved me dearly, he had the spirit of Peter. When I say that, I mean he cursed a lot as a child. He never cursed me, but outside of the presence of adults, you could always count on Terrell to share his feelings.

While in elementary school, he was known as a "teacher's pet". They adored Terrell! He was the highlight of the class because of how many talents he had. This made his mother proud. On the other hand, Terrell was so talkative that he often caused the class to be distracted. If he was not talking about me, he was talking about so many other things. He was so charming and had a smile that would warm the heart of the coldest soul. Due to his charisma and gift of gab, Terrell was able to get away with many things. As a young boy growing up in a single parent home with his mother and two sisters, he was not always as "masculine" as society and his family thought he should be. Though Terrell attended public schools, his mother Terrie decided to allow him to try private school, which was much better than public school. "Hey, Ms. Dobbins, can I go and play now?" asked Terrell. "Yes you can. You have been in time-out for fifteen minutes due to being disruptive in class. Don't let it happen again or the ruler will be your friend." she replied. Terrell was in the first grade at Immaculate Mary Catholic School where uniforms, discipline, and Christ-like behavior were the ideal. While Terrell was there, he had three best friends by the name of Khadijah, Casey and Rodriguez. These four were so much trouble once they were around each other in school. Terrell, while in the first grade had a crush on Casey, but kept it a secret. He did not understand at the time the significance of his feelings, but he became very close to Casey.

Now you might say, "He was just a child and he doesn't know any better." This statement is true especially when children are not aware of what sexuality is. He had never heard the terms homosexual, bisexual, gay, lesbian or any of the other words that describe persons of that lifestyle. I knew that from this point, Terrell would struggle because of his environment and what he had been exposed too. After Terrell finished catholic school, his mother had to take him out of school because it cost too much. Terrie worked several jobs in order to ensure that her three children had what they needed in order to survive. Being that Terrell was the baby of the group and the only boy, Terrie ensured that she protected her baby as much as she could.

She took him around to different places and raised him to be a respectable young man. Terrell and his father James were not close. When Terrell was born, his parents were not married. James was what they call, a rolling stone. For those of you who are confused, that means James was a womanizer. He loved women and women were his weakness. He dated Terrie and got her pregnant with Terrell. Following his birth, James noted that he did not want to be with Terrie. As many of you can probably attest, when the parents of children do not agree, the child is normally the one that suffers. Terrie always told Terrell that he could go and visit his father, but Terrell did not really have a desire to. He went with his dad on certain weekends. Terrell felt that his father was a good man, but later found that to be debatable.

Terrell went back to public school in Irvington, NJ where he was still a very bright child. His teachers loved him with the exception of one mean teacher that I allowed him to have in the second grade. Her name was Sylvia Vernon. Ms. Vernon talked much about me to the students, but she had such an evil spirit. I would always tell people even in today's society that if someone is proclaiming to be a follower of me, there is no way that they could be hateful and have a nasty spirit. Yes, change does come with time when a person is receptive to it; however, Ms. Vernon was seasoned. She should have changed years ago.

Ms. Vernon had to move Terrell's seat several times during the school year due to his talking. Finally, she had to place him right next to her, and that was a big mistake. This time, instead of Terrell talking to the students, he talked to her. Terrell was always finished with his work before everyone else, which is what allowed him to become such a busybody in the classroom. Ms. Vernon was so tired of Terrell that she moved his seat one last time about two rows in front of her desk. Terrell did comply, but he was not as innocent as most thought him to be. At the end of the year, children had to clean out their desk. During the end of the year, Terrell decided to be sneaky while cleaning out his desk. He had many broken crayons in his desk from the different activities that had been assigned that year. He decided to take the broken crayons and toss them over his shoulder in the direction of Ms. Vernon. He was instructed to take them to the trashcan, but he chose to do something different.

After about seven tossed crayons Ms. Vernon yelled, "Who in the hell is throwing crayons back here at me?" Terrell was very quiet, but his classmates told on him. He defended himself to the best of his ability, but Ms. Vernon was not listing to Terrell, and his gift of charisma did not save him this time. Terrell was very hardheaded. The only way to help some people is by letting them learn the hard way about breaking rules. Ms. Vernon pursued Terrell and grabbed him by his collar. She then proceeded to drag him to the back of the classroom where the broken crayons were and watched him pick them up. At this time, Terrell was in tears and Ms. Vernon was saying very disturbing things to him. He decided to go home that day and tell his mother. One thing about Terrie is that she believed everything her son said and in her eyes, Terrell was an angel. Terrie went to the school the next day and exchanged words with Ms. Vernon. When Terrell returned to class, Ms. Vernon provided him with a yellow sheet of paper and told him "You must write one hundred times I shall not lie". Terrell had to do what the teacher said and he learned from that point that his mother could not save him from everything. One thing in particular that his mother could not save him from was the verbal, physical, emotional, and mental abuse that her baby boy would receive.

While Terrell was back in public school, Terrell and his family had to move to his grandparents' house. Grandma Lilly and Granddad Lee had a big house and raised many people there throughout the years. One would think that with seven people living in a house that was "saved" life would be great. In this house, Terrell was exposed to many things such as pornography, which one of his uncles' watched religiously. This caused the mind of Terrell to mature much faster than needed.

"Hey Rell! What going on? I have a new game that I want to play with you!" said his cousin. Tyler and Terrell were 2 years apart. Terrell was seven and Tyler was nine.

"Sure Tyler! What kind of game is it?" said Terrell. The smirk that was on Tyler's face was one that seemed to be so gentle, but the meaning behind the smirk was devious.

"The game goes like this," said Tyler.

Terrell mostly played alone unless his favorite cousin Tyler came over to Grandma Lilly's house to play with him. Tyler would usually go to the backyard and reenact Power Rangers, by using a broom handle as his weapon and the trash can as his opponent. Other than that, Tyler played video games once he was done with his schoolwork. He also watched the soap operas with his mother and grandmother.

At this point Tyler and Terrell were in the basement of Grandma Lilly's house playing the video game until Tyler started to take off Terrell's clothes in an aggressive manner.

"Hey! What kind of game is this?" Terrell asked in confusion. "Why am I getting naked?"

"Because I said so," replied Tyler in an aggressive tone. "Now come here and lay down before I choke ya stupid ass!" Since Terrell was smaller than his cousin was, he listened to what his cousin said without hesitation due to the threat of his young innocent life at this time. Watching Terrell as he was in this state of confusion was hard for me, but I knew his end. I am not cruel, however, things make sense to individuals as they grow and mature.

As Terrell laid down on the cold basement floor naked and exposed, he could only think about Grandma Lilly being upstairs watching "Days of our Lives", when she should be down here monitoring this behavior. Grandma Lilly had no reason to suspect anything because children will be children and she figured that if anything had happened, someone would speak up about it. As Tyler began to touch Terrell in his private areas, the young boy was rendered helpless. He tried to tell Tyler to stop, however his favorite cousin did not comply. Terrell had his first sexual encounter at age 7.

The innocence of the young man was taken and he was in shock. He had never felt the pain as he felt that day of being violated. Terrell did receive whippings as a child due to punishment for bad behavior; however, he never experienced anything of this sort.

"Tyler and Terrell!" Grandma Lilly yelled down the stairs. Tyler jumped up and put his underwear on in fear that she was on her way down stairs while Terrell was still lying on the floor naked and violated. "Yall are too quiet down there. I do not hear any game. Bring ya asses up here now and go to the store and buy me some Marlboro Gold."

"Yes Ma'am. We are coming up soon. We just turned the volume down low so that we could hear you if you wanted us. We are coming up now." The door shut from where Grandma Lilly was calling.

"Put ya clothes on you fucking fag. You had better not tell no one what happened or I will kill you bitch! Every time that I come around, you already know what time it is. We are going to do this until I say it is done. I promise you. If you say one word, Aunt Terrie will not have a son anymore. You a little bitch anyway. You are not a thug. You don't act like a boy should." Those were the words that Tyler said as he walked away from Terrell and headed up the stairs dressed to go to the store for grandma. Terrell however was putting on his clothes in the cold basement crying because of the words that he had just heard as well as the experience.

"Why did this have to happen to me?" Terrell said sobbingly and he dragged his legs up the stairs to go and sit with grandma. "I don't understand,"

"What's wrong with you Terrell?" Grandma Lilly asked.

"Nothing, Grandma, my stomach just hurts a little bit."

Grandma Lilly proceeded to the kitchen and brought back a bottle of Castor Oil. "Here, take this spoonful and your stomach should be better after awhile."

It is amazing that in the homes of so many in today's society, the adults do not even know what is really going on with their children. Not understanding that when a child is afraid, they will not tell what is going on with them.

As time passed from the innocence of his youth, I watched Terrell struggle with his family and friends after the sexual acts began. One day, as Terrell was swinging on the gate at Grandma Lilly's house by himself in his solitude, his Uncle Jerome took his finger and put it up Terrell's butt through his clothes. Terrell jumped off the gate and looked at his uncle in confusion. Uncle Jerome then said, "You like that don't you, sweet boy!" Jerome laughed hysterically at his own nephew. Terrell stormed into his Grandmas' house where his other cousins were in the living room playing at the time.

"Here comes this fag mother fucker!" said his cousin Michael. The other four cousins all began to laugh and Terrell was very hurt.

He had no idea why his cousins would call him such a degrading name. At this time, Terrell knew what the derogatory comments meant due to the people that he grew up around, and his classmates at school.

"I am not a fag!" Terrell screamed at them in the living room. "Y'all stop calling me that! Fuck ya'll!" Tyler then got upset with Terrell and slapped him in the face. Terrell was not going to deal with this abuse and he fought back.

There in the living room, a brawl took place between Tyler and Terrell. Terrie came into the house, broke up the fight, and reprimanded her nephews who were making fun of her son. A mother's love is like no other. Then Terrell went into the attic, which was the room that he and his mother occupied since moving into the house.

There, Terrell began to sob and feel bad for them calling him these names. He was the one always picked on because he was different. He was always a good student, but because he was not "masculine" or into drugs, sports and other masculine things by the expectations of society, he was always labeled as an outcast or an outsider. Just as Terrell was sitting there crying, he heard footsteps coming up the attic stairs. He thought it was his mother, but instead he heard a voice say "Yo! You know what time it is!"

Terrell recognized that the voice was that of his cousin Tyler. Terrell was standing there wishing that he were never born. He began to take his clothes off and lay on the bed knowing that this was the time again for the molestation to continue.

From watching Terrell, I saw how hard his life was and I knew how hard his life would be because I made him. What he did not understand was that I equipped him for all of these trials before he was even born. The question was why did Terrell never speak up about this? The reason was that Terrell did not even know what was going on with himself and did not trust anyone in his family with information because there was no one who would understand.

This saddened me because even though I am a righteous judge, I am also merciful and my main ministry is that I love everyone. It was with love and kindness that I use to draw others. I am just a little perplexed that the church of today is not what I intended for it to be. They preach, persecute and destroy my people and they believe that I am pleased with that. I am not. Children are innocent as I created them until they are corrupted. Many lies occur in families and in the church because people do not want to face their own truth. They use my word to cover their issues and create bondage for others. I however, had Terrell go through these things so that I could raise him up to bring forth the truth.

As Terrell continued to go through mental, verbal, emotional and physical abuse, he still persevered in his life. I watched him through eyes that no one else could see but me, because I can see all. Terrell always knew that I loved him, so I thought, until he reached another pinnacle in his life called middle school. Terrell advanced to a magnet program for the musically inclined. Even though Terrell could not play sports, because his mother Terrie did not allow him to, he loved music and acting. He used to sing songs with his mother Terrie, who loved to sing Gospel music, and was a great soprano. He also sang R&B music with his sister Gabriel. Kelly Price was one of Gabriel's favorites, so Terrell became a fan as well. Music became his therapy, healing and strength especially during domestic violence disputes that his eyes endured as a child.

Granddad Lee was an alcoholic and would come home many days drunk. Although his grandmother would be praying when her husband came in drunk, this did not stop Lee's riots. He would come in the house cursing and beating on his wife. There were days that Terrell just had to sit and cry. There was nothing that he could do to stop the abuse. One day during a fight between Terrell's grandparents, one of his uncles that lived there, began to manhandle his dad. I was glad that someone finally stood up to him because the grandmother did not have enough strength to leave him. Contrary to popular belief, if you are a follower of me, do not stay in an abusive relationship and do not settle. Yes, I do allow things to happen in life; however, I always provide a way of escape. You can live a much better life without the abuse and the cost of your life.

During this time, Terrell became more active in his church, called

Temple Revival. It was located behind the projects and a senior citizen home. He grew up in this church, as did the rest of his family. While still in the innocence of his youth, he began to sing on the choir and play his clarinet, which he loved doing. It was during this time, at the age of 13, that Terrell had stopped being molested by his cousin Tyler. His mother and sisters moved to another part of town so that he could attend this magnet school.

Terrell was in the Music Magnet program for students who were musically inclined from grades 6-8. His mannerisms caused him again to be abused even in this new environment. One day in the cafeteria during his eighth grade year, Terrell and his best friend Alyssia were conversing and having a good time as they always had. Alyssia and Terrell connected in the 6th grade and were in the same class throughout middle school. Her family became his family—these foreigners talked fast, but cooked the most delicious food that the palate could have, according to Terrell.

One thing about Terrell was that I instilled in him the ability to give life and help others live, even when he did not believe that he was capable enough to do so. He always had a word and was liked amongst the majority. He was very charismatic, artistic, cunning, yet blunt. See, when people are abused, they form walls also known as defense mechanisms. In order for Terrell to not be labeled and abused as much, he began to show a hard exterior during middle school. He was very sharp with the tongue and would cut a person to pieces with his words before anyone could say anything to offend him. This was his only method of survival that he developed. He understood that his mother could not protect him from everything.

"Girl, let me tell you something," said Terrell to Alyssia while moving his head and swinging his hands in a feminine manner. "I do not have time to play with these little kids in this school. I am just tired of all of the hypocrites and I am ready to move on to high school. I just do not understand. Somebody needs to get them together or I will and they know it. I know that I am not perfect, but these kids are so damn immature. They talk about everyone and it's just really sad."

"Terrell you are a mess!" said Alyssia. "You're only 13 years old and you're talking like you are an old man. This is not anything new. You have always been that way and I love your face because of it."

"Well I have been through a lot at my tender age of 13," said Terrell "Growing up around all females, having no male figure to model myself after, and being ….well I do not need to talk about that. Anyways, are you excited about graduation? We are really growing up!" Terrell was the musical star of his class because he could sing and perform so well. He was excited because he had a solo at graduation.

Alyssia replied, "Yea I am happy! Next, we will be going to high school. Too bad we won't be in the same school."

"I know girl, but you know we will be best friends forever," said Terrell. "Whelp, it was good talking to you, but I have to attend to my business."

"Oh you are talking about Toya," said Alyssia sarcastically "You are obsessed with her."

"You know it," said Terrell in awe. "That is my boo. We have been dating all year and I am glad that we are going to the same high school. You know I love me some her. I really do like her a lot. She is the only girl besides my granny, mother and sisters that I can truly say that I love. I just hope that all works out with us. I want to marry her one day but she does not know that yet. So don't say anything."

There were many girls that wanted Terrell and that he dated during his time in middle school. Everyone always believed that Alyssia and Terrell would get married one day. Who knows what is to come of that situation? While having a good conversation and expressing his views on life, Terrell did have people who always had something negative to say outside of his family members. This young man named King, whom Terrell had been in school with since elementary, never saw eye to eye with him. King was a thug and lived the fast life. He was very macho and was popular because he was fresh. Not only did he dress the part, but he also had a way of getting what he wanted. He was an athlete and everybody loved an athlete.

During Terrell and Alyssia's conversation, King said loudly over his crowd of boys in the lunchroom, "LOOK AT THIS FAGGOT ASS MOTHER FUCKER! HE BEEN GAY SINCE ELEMETARY SCHOOL. HE TALK LIKE A SISSY, HE SWITCH AND PLUS HE BE WITH THE GIRLS ALL THE DAMN TIME. GROW SOME BALLS AND DO SOME MANLY STUFF FOR ONCE IN YOUR LIFE, GIRL!"

"BITCH, you know what...," replied Terrell now rising from his seat and conversation from Alyssia. "All of ya'll can kiss my big round ass...ALL OF MY ASS and go to hell! Ya'll do not know me, man...You just jealous because I have the girls and you do not. FUCK YOU, KING!" As Terrell stood up and King began to walk towards him, he began to see red. When Terrell was angry to the point of fighting, he saw red and in those moments, he became very dangerous. Terrell never really got in trouble in school and I wanted to make sure that he would not be in trouble now. Even in his rage, I began to place words in his spirit that said, "No weapon formed against me shall prosper. It won't work."

As King and the crowd walked off laughing, Terrell stood there angrily, watching them as they looked back and giggled. Terrell was angry because he could not seem to get away from the pain and the hurt of everyone calling him names. From his household, members of his church, to his school, there was constant abuse on the young man, but he always proved to be stronger because he was. I made him that way. I made him to be able to endure what the naysayers had spoken so that I could use him to prove them all wrong. Not for his glory, but for my glory. Everywhere Terrell went, they knew that he loved me because he talked about me often. Many youth do not talk about me because they do not know me. I was pleased to have such a great example as Terrell in the earth.

Alyssia stood up and touched his shoulder saying, "Don't let them dumb asses get to you. You know what you are. They do not have anything else to do but bother people who intimidate them. Many other boys act a lot worse than you do but they do not bother them. You have something that the rest of them don't have and that is God, plus you can sing."

"I just get tired of people calling me names all the time," said Terrell angrily. They always want to start trouble with me and I guess they mad cause I won't feed into their bull-shit...Lord knows I ain't got time."

Suddenly, the mood changed from a sense of rage and anger to deep sorrow. Life and death are in the power of the tongue and the words that are spoken, they are spirit and they are life. The negativity of the words had affected Terrell's spirit and he had been already battling on all sides, but no one knew this except for me and now Alyssia.

"I don't know what it means to be masculine. I have never had a man teach me. I do not know how to sag my pants, speak all of this slang talk, or even walk as a man is supposed to. What is wrong with the way that I talk to people? Yes, I do use my head and hands but that is just how I express myself." He began to cry. "I have always been different from everyone else.

That is not something that I can help. My uncles and cousins call me gay all the time. I always seem to be the joke of the family because I do not do the things that the other men do. I try to do things to fit in with people but I just cannot seem to do it. The harder I try, the more I feel like I am doing myself an injustice. I always pray and ask God why me...and I never get an answer. My mother tries her best to protect me, but there is only so much that she can do. She is stressed out and dealing with her own life issues. I cannot go and talk to her about it and my dad...we do not even have a good relationship. I do not believe that I can talk to him because he does not even express himself. I never hear how proud he is of me. I do not hear him say I love you. I do not even get a hug. I would believe that he cares, but I do not know. I just wish that life for me were different. I am doing all that I know how to at this time and it does not seem like it is enough. I am thirteen. Puberty is hitting. My hormones are raging and people just do not understand what I go through on a day-to-day basis. I just feel alone most of the time."

Alyssia replied, "Well people will be people, Terrell. Just do not worry about it. Everything will work out. Hell! We all are still young. We still have our whole lives for things to make sense. Just let things come to you as time goes on. You are still a great young man and everyone mostly in the school from the administration on down to us as students know you and love you for the real dude that you are! Now stop crying boy. You need to go see Toya and get ready for graduation practice. You know you have to lead that song. When you sing, I feel Jesus even when you do not sing a Gospel song. So clean yourself up and let us go. I am always here for you."

Once Terrell wiped his eyes, he hugged Alyssia and said, "Yea you are right, Alyssia. Thanks! I love you, girl!"

One thing about me is that I will always place a voice of reason in your life. You just have to be attentive and listen to me as I speak through others to relay messages to you.

During this time of turmoil, and what seemed to be defeat, I was always with Terrell. He and I would talk everyday and he knew me as I knew him. We would talk for hours and hours at a time. We would have good conversations. I have always spoken to him and he has always heard me despite what was going on in his life! He was still growing and maturing so I could not push him too fast to do too much because I did not want him to crack under pressure.

I will never put more on a person than they can handle. When he would ask me questions, I did not always give him an answer. He would not understand at this age what was taking place. He would not understand that what was coming for him would be so much greater than where he was now. As any parent or true friend does, I kept my mouth shut because this was something that he would just have to take one day at a time, learn, gain understanding, and apply the life lessons later on in life.

Eighth grade graduation was so great for Terrell. He finished strong and learned a lot about his gift of singing and acting. While he was in middle school, he met lifelong friends. Terrell would prove to be the one who helped them all stay strong in their relationships with me.

Terrell led a song called "Like an Eagle" at graduation. During that time, the entire school went to a nearby community college for their graduation ceremony. As he sang, he saw his family in the stands and the Principal of the school, Dr. N. Holloway, who was always very pleased with Terrell. She always acknowledged his potential in all that he did and accomplished. He also saw his mentor, Mr. Kris who was a member of Phi Beta Sigma. He was his mentor all through middle school and Terrell was a member of the Beta Club that Mr. Kris was supervising. Mr. Kris served as Terrell's father figure and taught him how to tie his first tie and guide him on what it was like to be an African American male. Yes, it is rough not to have positive biological parents, but I will always send in people that can help you develop in the areas that you are lacking guidance as well as support. You just have to be receptive of whom I am sending and what they have been sent in your life to accomplish.

As Terrell began to sing, he then began to minister. He began to speak life to the people making sure that they knew that they could fly above the highest obstacles and succeed in all areas of their lives. People loved to hear Terrell sing because he was highly anointed. When he sang, things happened and lives were changed. What Terrell did not know was the song that he was leading was prophetic for him. He had no idea that the trials that he had faced thus far and would face in the future would cause him to fly like an eagle and to soar above the storms of life and not come down until the climate was conducive.

This had proven to be a great day. Terrie's baby boy graduated, which was a blessing. His father was present as well as his two sisters. As he proceeded to leave the auditorium, he wished his friends well and prayed God's blessing be upon them all as they prepared to enter into the journey of high school.

"Terrell, I am going to miss you so much!" said Alyssia. "We live in the same city so just make sure that you come and see me and tell mom I said hello."

"Girl, you know I got you," replied Terrell. "I wish you the best in that prestigious high school that you are going to attend in Montclair. Don't let them people turn you out or I am going to kick your ass!"

They both laughed and embraced for the final time for that moment. Alyssia and Terrell had such a strong relationship and he was devastated that Alyssia could not travel to Frank Morrell High with him.

After graduation, Terrell and Toya talked almost every day on the telephone. Terrell was happy to have Toya in his life. She was a little rough around the edges, but she was beautiful amongst many other things. He shared his first real kiss with Toya. They were truly in love at a young age and I was happy for their present.

It is always the job of the evil one to try to destroy such greatness, that I have created. Therefore, I spoke these words to Terrell from his birth and I am speaking it again in his time of trouble, because high school was just the beginning.

"I am your shepherd; you shall not want. I maketh you to lie down in green pastures: I leadeth you beside the still waters. I restoreth your soul: I leadeth you in the paths of righteousness for my name's sake. Yea, though you walk through the valley of the shadow of death, you will fear no evil: for I am with you; my rod and my staff, they comfort you. I prepareth a table before you in the presence of your enemies: I anointeth your head with oil; your cup runneth over. Surely goodness and mercy shall follow you all the days of your life: and you will dwell in my house forever." Psalms 23

I gave him a command that even in all that he saw and endured in the world as well as church, he would always be in my house. I did not tell him why at that time nor reveal the other parts of his calling, but as long as he knew that I was leading him, he would be all right if he lived and moved according to my will and my way for his life. No one fully knows my thoughts nor understands my ways. I am a mystery. This makes me worth seeking, which is what Terrell did. I have shown him things in dreams and he was able to speak my oracles. Even though he did not understand them, he knew that he was special to me and that I would use him to do great things in the earth.

CHAPTER 3
Transitions

"Lord I hear you talking to me," Terrell wrote in his journal during 3rd period. "I am doing what I can now. I am in high school! I made it! This is great! I am with my boo Toya and all is well. I just do not believe that I made it to this point! Really! I am a freshman in high school. This is not where I want to be. I strongly desired to attend Performing Arts High School, but I guess it was not in your will for me to be there. Therefore, I am just going to make the best of this bad situation. I am going to do my best in high school. Many people have attended Frank Morrell High School and have been successful. I do not know what to expect, but all I know is that you have been with me in times past and I know that you will be with me now. Thank you, Lord, for doing all things."

There were individuals from Terrell's family that attended the same high school including his sister Gabriel. Gabriel was very feisty and a fighter. There was one day that Terrell and his mother Terrie had to go to the school and get Gabriel because she was in a huge dispute with some other females. This was scary for Terrell to watch because his sister was so enraged. This particular high school was the only one in the city. As you can imagine, most urban city schools are challenging. High poverty, low-income, crime, gangs, sex, drugs, and death are what normally occur in these areas. Even though Terrell was raised in the ghetto, I did not allow him to be totally conformed to his environment.

As he proceeded to attend Frank Morrell High, he was very nervous. Attending a school that had close to one thousand students was very intimidating. As we remember from the previous chapter, Terrell was abused on multiple levels due to his lack of masculinity. During his first year in high school, Terrell went through the typical change that a teenager might encounter (as it pertains to peer pressure). Terrell did not have a sense of fashion while he was in middle school because he wore uniforms. However, in high school, his appearance became more important to him. Thus, Terrell decided to play the safe role in order to minimize the effect of bullying. He wore very baggy jeans to school, and alternated between white and black colored extra large t-shirts every week. He even tried to change his walk to fit what society deemed to be thuggish. Terrell did his best to fit in with the new school environment. Even in his outward change, his heart and spirit were still the same.

Terrell, during his first year of high school, gained favor with the entire administration. Some of the people that worked at his high school had also worked at his middle school in previous years. Because Terrell was so talented, he did not maintain the image of a thug for a long time. He joined a program called Multipot Dance Company. Being a member of this dance troupe allowed him to express himself in an artistic manner as he had always done. He danced in the forms of African, swing and modern dance. Along with that, he enhanced the music component of the organization by creating a music group called "Da Truth". This group consisted of five members. One of which was a friend from middle school named Shanae Cruz. As mentioned before, Terrell was a little rough around the edges. He would tend to speak without thinking first. Anything that was on his mind came out of his mouth. Terrell did not really care much for Shanae when she first entered into his music magnet class in middle school because she was tall with big feet and short hair. It was not until she opened up her mouth and sang "Home" from The Wiz that he fell in love with her spirit.

Now, this does sound harsh, but Terrell was a really harsh, yet loving individual. From that point forward, Shanae and Terrell became good friends. Older people loved Terrell because they were fascinated with his love for God and his maturity. One of these people that loved him was Ms. Cruz. She was the mother of Shanae. They became very close and Terrell looked to Ms. Cruz as being another mother to him until she passed away. Due to the relationship that they had, Terrell felt inclined to minister in song at the funeral of Ms. Cruz in which Shanae was grateful. This is another reason why she was one of the original members of the group that Terrell established.

During Terrell's first year, he was involved with many other programs that helped him develop into being a young man including additional time in the Beta Club. Terrell's mother worked as a teacher with little children and she was always proud of her only son, her boy, Terrell. He decided to become involved with additional plays and productions. He decided to audition for the African Globe Theater and he was the star of additional productions. He starred in musicals such as, Dreamgirls, Black Nativity, Gospel at Colonus, and Macbeth in the Hood. With all of these accolades and accomplishments at such a young age, one would think that Terrell was prepared for his high school experience. Contrary to popular belief, just because things seem to be wonderful, it does not mean that there will not be challenges that surprise you in life.

You know, it is so funny that when all things are going well, people tell me how good I am but when things go wrong they are so quick to lose faith in me, when I know all things and have been there all the time. I really do have to laugh at myself sometimes, because the people that I have created are just comical. As I watched and guided Terrell through his first year in high school, he had no idea what he was going to face upon leaving the cafeteria that day. As he proceeded to go to his locker, which was on the third floor of Frank Morrell High School, he figured that he would go to see his girlfriend Toya. Her locker was on the other side of the building and as Terrell was turning the corner happily to see his boo since middle school, he saw the back of Toya's head. As he proceeded to turn completely, he also noticed that Toya's arms wrapped around the neck of another male by the name of Nigel. Nigel was a senior at Frank Morrell and was in the Beta Club with Terrell. Nigel had no idea that Terrell and Toya were actually dating. In fact, Nigel always said he considered Terrell to be his little twin brother. Even though Nigel did not know that he was dating Toya, he still felt betrayed by the both of them.

Terrell stepped back with shock and his face twisted in disgust. Toya then proceeded to kiss Nigel without knowing that Terrell was right behind her. Nigel pointed in Terrell's direction after their passionate kiss and Toya turned around suddenly with a look of surprise.

"I am sorry, Terrell," she said. "I have been seeing Nigel for a few months. You are just too passive and feminine acting for me. I needed something else in my life like a real man and I do not view you as being that. Yes, you are willing to do anything for me and you have not pressured me into even having sex with you as some others have since being here during our first year of high school. You are very talented and I know that you would do better finding someone else that cares for you as much as you care for them. I hope this does not cause any hard feelings. I still love you and all but, I do not want to be with you anymore. You are just not, what I am looking for anymore. It was nice while in middle school, but that time is over."

While telling Terrell this, his mouth was wide open as he tried to digest what he had seen and heard. Can you imagine having whom you thought was the love of your life; drop a bomb like that on you? Let us remember, this is the only girl that Terrell really did love outside of the women in his family. He was planning to marry Toya, the one who had stolen his heart.

In times of heartache, the door of the spirit becomes open which allows people to become vulnerable. Terrell had never experienced true love, so he did not know how to respond to this situation without being condescending and rude. He used these mechanisms to protect his heart, which had been shattered from childhood, by many people who also claimed to love him.

Terrell became enraged! "You nasty Bitch!" he yelled. "You could have just told me that is what you wanted. You know what? Fuck You, Bitch! How in the hell would you do something like this to me? You act as if you do not even care. I see high school has turned you into a whore already and we just got here. Fuck you, Toya!"

Nigel stepped up and he and Terrell began to argue, but there was no fight because Terrell and Nigel were both in the high school Beta club. Terrell and Nigel would not fight because one of the key principles of the Beta Club was brotherhood. Outside of this issue with Toya, Nigel was actually becoming the older brother that Terrell wished that he had. Toya stood in between them, but she made it clear she was on Nigel's side. Terrell took a couple of steps back and then stormed off in the opposite direction before the bell rang for dismissal.

I began telling Terrell that he needed to calm down, but by this time, he was too hurt to listen and his heart too heavy to be lifted. He had lost the one thing that he loved and felt loved him back, and it just crushed his heart.

If you take a hammer to glass, the result is what Terrell's heart resembled. Life will always be worse when people do not want to listen to me, especially when they are acting out of hurt. I have endured a lot more hurt than that, but I still hear the cries of the people and answer them. If I can endure affliction, death, hell and the grave, surely Terrell can endure this.

After the incident, Terrell was furious for a long time, but I softened his heart as much as he would allow me to. A few weeks had passed from the springtime of Terrell's first year and I listened to him as he started talking to me again. He was not mad at me for the incident that occurred, but I knew Terrell. When he got mad, he did not talk to anyone. He always bottled things in, and this is what caused him to have such a bad temper. It never took much to strike Terrell's attitude. Since I know all, he decided to talk to me about the situation because I gave him a part of me that would give him comfort in his times of distress. Since he was so hurt and vulnerable, he left himself open to embrace another side of him that he had kept suppressed under his love for Toya.

A nugget of wisdom to parents that are raising children. Pay attention to your children and their behavior. Adolescent and teenage years are very pivotal and influential times for children. You should be having honest conversations with your children about life and sexuality whether you are a follower of me or not. Children will learn a lot on their own, which is fine, but when I have placed you in their lives, do not be afraid to have the hard conversations. So many of your children are walking around with secrets and feelings that they do not know how to express. This is what causes many youth to commit suicide, because they have no one to talk to, or feel as though they will be condemned. Do not use me as a way to send people to the hell that I did not intend for them to enter especially when I and no one else order their lives.

Terrell had known that he was attracted to guys since he was younger. Due to his upbringing in the church, this is something that he never expressed with anyone and he wanted to keep it that way. He was very active in church, and sang with different gospel groups in the area. As a teenager, he did not know what the response would be if he started to explore what he had been feeling for so many years.

CHAPTER 4
The Open Wound

Months had passed and it was now summer going into his sophomore year of high school. Terrell had a lot of time to think about his first year of high school, and people whom he had met. He had to understand that the love of his life did not love him in the same way. He figured if it were meant to happen, it would happen in the future. During his time of reflection, he remembered the good times and the bad. One of the memories that Terrell thought to be hilarious was getting high for the first time. While Terrell was in gym class one day with one of his new friends, Patricia, he was tricked. People have the tendency to practice bad habits during their time of trouble. In his time of trouble, Terrell smoked Black & Mild cigars. He did not know how to loosen the tobacco, so he asked his friend Patricia to do it. While she was sitting in the bleachers outside on the field, Terrell was speaking with some of his other friends while Patricia loosened the tobacco.

Once Patricia was finished, she and Terrell opted to indulge in smoking the cigars. They went through four cigars in less than forty-five minutes. After gym class was Spanish with Ms. K, who was a very laid-back teacher who loved Terrell. Patricia, on the other hand, was not one of her favorite students because she would talk about sex all the time during class. As they entered the classroom, everything became comical for Patricia and Terrell. He could not understand why everything was so funny and why he would make so many loud jokes in class. Terrell had never been the class clown, but on this day, he was and could not control it. He always had a sense of humor, but this was extreme and Ms. K was not pleased with this activity.

"Terrell! I don't know what has gotten into you," said Ms. K in her stern Spanish accent. "But if you don't stop this behavior, I am going to call your mother," Once Terrell heard that his mother would be contacted, he straightened up fast because he did not want to get embarrassed by Terrie.

After sixth period was over, Patricia decided to tell Terrell that she had laced his Black & Mild with weed. Even though Terrell was shocked that Patricia did this to him, he laughed hysterically at the fact that he smoked weed and did not know it. He had good times with his friend Patricia, but there was one person that caught his attention that he did not expect would ever approach him.

One day while walking in Franklin Center, thinking about his life, and looking for some new music, he ran into one of his friends from school named Prince. Prince and Terrell were on the Gospel Choir together since his first year of high school. As they passed, Terrell noticed that Prince gave him a look that was a little strange, but did not pay it much attention at that time. Terrell had the tendency to not pay people any mind that he thought could be interested in him.

Now that it was going into sophomore year of high school, Terrell was just dealing with many issues. He was tired of his mother Terrie and her stressful behavior. Being a single parent and having no one else to take her frustrations out on besides Terrell, since he was the only child left in the house, she took them out on him. Terrell's mother had many issues and did not have the best relationship with her only son Terrell at this particular time and they did not talk much as Terrell began to deal more with his personal life. He did not fully trust his mother with very personal things because he was fearful that she would go and tell the rest of the family.

One time, Terrell had an infection and just because he did not tell his mother what it was, she went and told the family that he could possibly have an STD. This is just like many parents who assume the worst when their child chooses not to talk. Now, Terrie was not a bad parent at all. She loved her son and would do anything for him, but this was her first boy. Raising a son is different than raising a daughter. Males normally have more stored emotions and must feel comfortable without being judged. Terrell was just tired of going through hardships and being hurt by people who allegedly loved him.

As you are reading this, I am sure that you can recall times in your life where you have felt and experienced the exact thing that Terrell was feeling. Ironically, one day Prince came along, approached Terrell randomly, and said, "Yo I like you."

Terrell looked at Prince and said to himself, "What the hell?"

"Ok," he said, "That is nice, I guess. I like you too. You cool." He said this because he saw how consistent Prince was with him and how they came to bond together. People look for consistency in individuals. Even though this is a good trait to have, certain people are only consistent as long as there is a benefit in their relationship, even if this means using a person and holding secret motives.

Prince then proceeded to ask a very invasive question while smirking. "So you want to be my boyfriend?"

Terrell then began thinking about his attraction to males, the number of years that the molestation occurred, the deception of his love Toya, and yearning for love. Being involved with a guy was all that he knew how to do, but he was still confused. Terrell had other girlfriends throughout the years that he liked, but the truth is he always had another attraction. He remembered when he was in the first grade how he had a crush on Casey, one of his classmates. At that time and being that young, Terrell did not know, what it was that he was feeling. He then replied to Prince "I don't get down like that, man."

This is something that Terrell had been fighting for a very long time. He did not know how to understand another male liking him, and he always lived in condemnation because the church preached about it being wrong and that he would go to hell if he participated in such activity or acknowledged his feelings for a member of the same sex. Was Terrell a homosexual after all? Were the allegations of his family, church and classmates true? How do you think a teenager would be feeling at this time? I will tell you the answer. Very vulnerable!

Prince then proceeded to kiss Terrell. Terrell never experienced the emotions that rushed through him at that time. He had kissed Toya before and other girls while he was younger but this feeling was different. Chills went down his spine and his body felt what he thought to be good at that time.

Terrell was astonished at this point and could not say anything. He did say to himself, "What in the hell just happened? That is so nasty, but felt so right. Jesus, I need you to help me. This is not right."

Prince walked away smiling and said, "I will see you tomorrow in school!"

Terrell smiled and went home thinking about what had just taken place and he did not know what to do.

Terrell contemplated what was going on, mostly because he knows that in my word this behavior is not favorable in my sight, based on what he only knew on paper. He was used to church bashing, or "Hate Theory," as I call it in the church; but this was a time for Terrell to stop pushing aside how he felt and who he was because of church people. He knew how they saw him, but not how I see him. You can never please people and they hide behind so many masks. I am not a ruthless God; I am a righteous judge. I would never allow things to happen just to send people to hell and what people fail to realize is that I take the foolish things and inappropriate things in order to get the glory. It is amazing how people think that they have me figured out.

From there, some weeks passed and then, in September of Terrell's sophomore year, they became a couple. Yes! Terrell began dating Prince. A male! This was Terrell's first relationship with a guy and he was happy— so he thought. They spent a lot of time together, did a lot of things and Terrell had really grown to love Prince because of his charm, ability to sing, and his spirituality. Being that Terrell was so young, he engaged in behavior that was not wise. In his high school, they did not teach much on STD's nor HIV/AIDS. Terrell had sexual experiences with Prince, unprotected on many occasions and did not think anything of it, until he found out some disturbing news about his boyfriend. One day while at Frank Morrell High, Terrell was walking on the first floor and saw Prince talking with someone by the name of Juan. Prince was touching Juan inappropriately in the hallway and Terrell was looking at them with a puzzled look. Once Juan saw Terrell, he rolled his eyes and Prince turned around towards Terrell.

"Hey boo," said Prince with his large charming smile. It is good to see you,"

"Who the hell is that you hugged up on, Prince?" replied Terrell in a nasty tone.

"That is just Juan," replied Prince. "He is all right. You just don't need to talk to him because he does not like you."

"Well that is fine," said Terrell as he and Prince walked away. "Many people do not like me. He can join the club of haters that I have."

As time progressed, Terrell caught Prince trying to kiss Juan, but he never said anything. At this time, Terrell knew that charming Prince was also a charming liar. He proceeded one day to approach Juan while he was at his locker alone.

"Hey Juan. How are you?" said Terrell.

Juan was more feminine acting than Terrell. "Hello, Terrell," he replied sarcastically. "I am fine. And you?"

"Let me just cut the bullshit," replied Terrell. "I have seen you and my boyfriend together way too much. What is going on? Prince told me that you did not like me and to stay away from you."

"He told you what?" stated Juan while laughing. "Why would he tell you that I did not like you? I do not even know you like that. The truth is your man has been trying to get back with me and he has been having sex with the band director and other people in this school. You are not his priority."

Terrell was astonished by what he heard. Not only was he astonished, he was hurt by the fact that he had another person in his life that was lying to him and using him. From their continued dialogue, Juan and Terrell realized that the same person was playing them both. They decided to confront Prince in front of the school with a sock full of quarters and a brawl.

When Prince came outside after school, Juan and Terrell were standing next to each other. Terrell had the sock of quarters in his right hand and they were ready to beat the daylights out of Prince. Once Prince saw them, he knew that he was in trouble and ran back into the school alerting the security guards that there were people outside waiting to harm him. Juan became rowdy at this time, but he and Terrell both left the school and became good friends. Juan had two other friends named Marcus and Corey that Terrell had seen around school, but was not friends with at the time. Terrell then became friends with the "rainbow crowd".. Now Terrell had someone else who was like him, who he could talk to and not feel as though he was all alone in the world.

It is now December and Terrell is a very different person. He was still facing the fact that the boy that he had feelings for was cheating on him. He also had to face the fact that he had befriended openly gay feminine males, and he now hung around them during the day at school. Everyone in high school began to find out about Terrell once he began to hang around the gay crew, but Terrell did not really care because he was comfortable with himself. However, Terrell was still trying to find himself - his life began to do a downward spiral. In the midst of him trying to find himself, he lost his way. He began cutting class to do meaningless things, like take the train to New York during school hours, and watching hours of pornography.

To cope with the struggles of his life, he listened to music. Two of his favorite CD's were from Destiny's Child: Destiny Fulfilled, which came out after his breakup with Prince; as well as Fantasia: Free Yourself who was a winner of the television show, *American Idol.* These songs became life to him, as he listened to the lyrics in order to become free from the soul tie that he had with Prince. Even though this was a difficult task, this was not the most challenging during the latter part of 2004. With that drama going on in Terrell's life, he became very depressed, but he did not talk to anyone about his problems, due to his fear of judgment. He did not even talk to me as much as he used to.

In December of that same year on a Saturday morning, Terrell was at home and went in the living room of the one-bedroom apartment to talk to his mom, whom he loved dearly, despite her negative ways, and heard his sisters in the living room.

"Mom! What you doing today?"

His mother did not respond, but his sisters greeted Terrell by saying hello and hugging him. "Why do you want to know what I am doing, faggot?" said Terrell's' mother. "You go and ask your boyfriend Prince what he is doing? I went through your phone last night while you were sleeping and I saw some old text messages that you were sending to each other!" Terrell stopped in his tracks, as he was heading back to the bedroom, and turned around to face his mother.

"What did you just call me?" He said in anger. This astonished Terrell because he had heard the word faggot from his cousins, uncles and other people, but never from his mother. He was really in shock because he wondered how in the world, and why someone who had birthed him into the world, would not ask questions, but instead automatically say something negative to their own child; say something that he had heard all of his life; say something that he didn't know how to deal with?

Then there was silence in the room. Terrell's sisters tried to justify him and tell their mother that nothing of that nature was going on. The sisters were significantly older than Terrell so they had no idea what happened to Terrell or what he was dealing with. Terrell's mother at this time did not even bother to look him in his face.

Once they left, the brawl between mother and son was like no other. Words exchanged and I was just looking down on them understanding how both of them were feeling, but I could not change the situation because it was necessary for them.

Towards the end of the argument, Terrell yelled at his mother saying,

"Since you think that I am a faggot and you won't give me any privacy, then I am moving out. I am going to stay with daddy. Even though he was not there to raise me because of you and your attitude, I know that he would never come out and call me nothing like that to my face. And yet you wonder why your other two kids don't want to stay with you!"

That was on a Saturday and the house was very quiet until that Wednesday of the same week. Terrell was gone and moved in with his father at age of 15. Even though he did not raise him, he did come around to check on his son. The only thing that his father did was pay his child support at the end of the month since Terrell was born. He would also take him on occasional trips to play the lottery in New York.

Now that Terrell was 15 years old and a sophomore in high school, he was having an identity crisis and had no one to talk to but me. His grades had dropped significantly and it did not seem like anyone cared about what he was going through. He figured that at this point in his life, he needed a human being to talk to about this, but did not trust anyone. He did not believe that people would understand his struggles. He knew that he liked the same sex but could not tell anyone because of fear that he would not be accepted.

One day, a young woman whom Terrell considered his God sister named Ashley called him. "Hey brother. You have been heavy in my spirit and my Godmother who attends different services that we have sung at has had her eye on you and wants to talk to you." "Ok. That is fine I guess," replied Terrell. He did not know that I sent help in his time of distress, but it was great that this conversation happened. While Terrell was on hold, he heard another woman's voice on the other side of the phone that was not Ashley. She said, "Hello Terrell, my name is Evangelist Carry Harold and the Lord has been speaking to me about you. He told me to minister to you, because you are suffering from major depression, and that spirit is trying to kill you so that you will not reach the place that God has for you. You are a great man and the enemy wants to attack your mind, but I am here on assignment from God to deliver and set you free!"

As they continued to talk on the phone, Terrell did nothing but cry because all this time, he was not sure if I was really listening to him, but I was all along. I had sent her to help him walk into his calling. That phone conversation lasted over 2 hours and Terrell was still battling with all the events of life. He had still not told anyone that he liked the same sex, and it began to depress him even more, which caused him to feel helpless and hopeless.

A week before Christmas of that same year in that same month that he argued with his mom, moved in with his father, broke up with his first boyfriend, and was having trouble expressing himself; Terrell took what he thought would be the last stand of life. One night, he was crying in the one bedroom apartment, in which his Dad slept in the living room while Terrell had the bed, in the apartment on the other side of town from his mother's house. He was so heavy and did not think that life was going to get any better. I am sure that as you are reading this, it should cause you to reflect over your own life, but also should provoke you to talk to your children if you have any and for the youth, talk to someone about your problems.

"Lord, I just don't understand what is going on," Terrell began. "How am I going to deal with this when no one will understand? No one thinks that I will make it in life especially being that I am like this. I do not even think that I can make it. I am sure that I cannot!

You already hate me because I am this way so if you hate me, and everyone else will once I tell them, then I might as well just not be! Why is this so wrong? Why do I feel so bad? I did not ask to be like this. Why am I like this? I cannot take this anymore. I do not know what to do!

"I do not have the power to overcome this anymore. I have been dealing with this too long. No one will ever understand. I cannot tell the people in my church I am like this because they preach down against being homosexual or bisexual.

Well Lord if this is so wrong, then why would you make me this way? Why would you let all of this stuff happen to me? I am still young! I want to live a normal life like the rest of the young people who are my peers. However, here I am, living this life in condemnation and not happy with my life nor myself. I have not talked to my mother in a long time, and I cannot talk to anyone else.

You know what? This is it. Fuck this. Fuck this life. I am out of here. I do not want to live anymore and no one loves me anyway. I will not be missed because people don't really care about me."

Terrell then decided to stand on the ledge of the window. Seven stories up, I watched him mark his place where he planned on landing after he jumped to commit suicide. Suicide was the only way that he believed would solve the issues of life.

I watched him crying out on the ledge and I saw the demons and the spirit of death hovering around him but they were not on him, because I had a hedge to protect him, since before he was born and my blood covered him. During this time, I said to myself that it is now time to move in and let Terrell know that he would make it past this despite what he felt and what others said. Therefore, I got up off my throne and came down to talk to him face to face. As I appeared to him, I was the only light in all of the darkness in his life.

I came right in front of his face and I said to him "Lo, I am with you even until the ends of the Earth. You may not understand what is going on now, but you will in due season. I love you for who you are and I have chosen, called, anointed and appointed you to do great things in my name. No one else can do what you do because I have not assigned it to him or her but I have assigned it to you. Your life will be great and you will be what I have called you to be despite what people have said and will continue to say. Get off this ledge. Go back in the room and cry out for deliverance. I am here with you to deliver you and most of all, I LOVE YOU!" Then I came back up to the heavens to watch what was to take place, even though I already knew.

Terrell then got off the ledge, went back into the bedroom and prayed unto me like never before. It was during this private moment that I filled him with the Holy Spirit. It always helps people when I show up during their least expected time. I would never just leave ones who I have called, and chosen to die for, due to life's circumstances. I would be evil if I did that, and I am the opposite of evil. I am full of love and compassion. I seek willing vessels so that I can use them effectively.

I heard Terrell cry out for me to save him and to deliver him. In the midst of his tears and crying out unto me, I delivered him from that bondage. They that sow in tears, shall reap in joy. He then was blessed to speak in an unknown tongue, but I understood all that he was saying. I am a witness, that when you are truly free from the things that bind you, you will rejoice.

From that day forward, Terrell and I became closer. He began to trust me more and build relationship with me. Because he acknowledged me first in all his ways, I was now able fully to direct his path. I will make the foolish things confuse the wise. Yes, people were saying that Terrell should have done this and should have done that, but I have allowed all things to work together for his good. Terrell then became accepting of what he was dealing with and began to share this with his close friends. Some were upset like two of his close male friends Kroy and Emmanuel, but others did not have a problem with his sexuality because they understood that sexuality is not a choice. They received him with open arms and loved him as I would, and I do, without standing in a seat of judgment. Some of them also said to him "Terrell, I knew that a long time ago." This statement did offend Terrell a little, but he always laughed because it was funny. He and Shanae became very close after his confession because she too was the same way. It is not as if Terrell was a bad person because he was not. He was loving, brutally honest, anointed, compassionate, saved, sanctified, holy ghost filled, and a go-getter just to name a few of his characteristics.

As the year of 2004 was ending, another Gospel artist that helped him press through his hard times was Byron Cage. He had a CD out at that time and it ministered life into Terrell. Now, in the new year of 2005, during the spring, Terrell did engage in another relationship with a male whom was 13 years older than he was. It was nice, however due to obvious circumstances; the relationship did not last as long. His name was Neil and he was a loving man whom Terrell did learn a lot from and would prove to be a faithful friend throughout the years. Neil had his own place. Terrell was living with his dad and did whatever he wanted to do. He would spend nights at Neil's house and turn his phone off not understanding the anguish that his parents were in not knowing where their child was. However, as most teenagers that have been through a lot, adults could not tell Terrell anything. He knew it all, so he thought.

I then began to show him his calling more in depth as far as him preaching the Gospel. He has a sound in his mouth that can destroy the bondage of the enemy. During this time in 2005, Terrell was still actively attending Temple Revival. He began to sing on the Praise and Worship team, where he became a praise and worship leader. He learned what it really meant to minister out of an authentic place from relationship. He was skillful and anointed. Being active in ministry kept Terrell busy, and his life began to change for the better. During one particular service, Evangelist Harold prayed for him, and his life changed drastically. He began following her in ministry and became one of her Godsons, which made him very happy.

To Terrell's surprise, while he was living with his dad, his parents began conversing again outside of checking on him. During the summer of 2005, his parents decided that after 15 years of not dating, but producing the "unplanned son" that they would get married. Terrell was not pleased with this decision, as he had not fully forgiven his mother for what she had done, but his leaving caused them to reunite. Terrell told his parents that I was not pleased with their union and that their relationship would not last. They did not believe him. They should have, because I was speaking to them, prophetically through him. The evening before they got married, Terrell's dad James Turner lost his mother. The next day Terrell told them it was a sign from me that they should not get married. Again, being disobedient, they were married and had to travel to Florida for the funeral services of his grandmother. Terrell did not know his father's side of the family and had only visited Florida one time. During this time, I began to use Terrell much prophetically. He did not understand fully what was going on, but he knew my voice and we began to spend a lot of time together. Moving into his junior year, I did not like the change that happened to him.

CHAPTER 5
Preaching Hate

Junior year had arrived and Terrell was on fire because he felt as though, what he had endured to this point made him invincible. He felt as though he was on top of the world, and that he could save the world. Terrell was always a very spiritual and deep person, so as he began to go to church more consistently, reading the Bible, and praying, I was able to show myself to him in a great way. This was so phenomenal! I felt so appreciated at this point, and I was proud of Terrell because he had chosen to seek me in all of his ways. Even though he was still struggling with his sexuality, he made a decision not to engage in sexual activity, and felt as though he had been delivered. He felt as though he had become a perfect being. See, the problem with most people is that just because you experience an ounce of freedom does not mean that you have fully escaped bondage. A person can be free from a place of bondage physically, but remain captive in the mind.

If we could rewind for a minute, I would like to share an important fact about Terrell with you. While in high school during his sophomore year, Terrell became very involved with his guidance department. His high school guidance counselor was the same counselor that his sister Gabriel had when she attended there.

"Terrell, you are totally different from your sister with the exception of your attitude," " said Momma West. "Both of you are so feisty.

Terrell called her Momma West because she was like another mother to him. She would encourage him and then curse him out at the same time. Terrell would cut class many days in the guidance office, but he never got in trouble because of the favor on his life.

One day, Terrell was introduced to this tall woman named Sandra Hunter who was a friend of Momma West.

"Sandra, this is Terrell," said Momma West. "He is one of my brightest students and he has a calling on his life,"
Terrell thought to himself, "Alright. I do not know who she is. What relevance is she to my life?"

"Greetings, Mrs. Hunter," he said. "It is nice to meet you. What is your occupation?" "I work for the township of Irvington and do many other things," she replied. "I love working with the youth and I have a mentorship program for young ladies."

They continued their dialogue and over the course of a few months, Mrs. Hunter had become one of his mentors. I established this divine connection.

As Terrell and Ms. Hunter became closer over time, Terrell inquired about her starting a program for males. The program would consist of leadership and development, because the high school did not have that type of program. Thus, the Irvington Diplomats was born, and only the elite young men of the high school were accepted into the program. During this time, I allowed Terrell to see that his vision for things could happen if he was only connected to the right people. The program became a success and gained much recognition, not just in the high school, but also in the township at large. So many positive things were coming about and Terrell's ego was boosted.

During his junior year, Terrell decided to be baptized at Temple Revival. He felt the pull to be born again. In my word, I do talk about being born again. Yes, you are born of humanity, but to be born again, you must be born of the spirit. Terrell's desire was to be born of the spirit and no longer chase after the flesh, and other appealing things of life. He believed that those who were in ministry were perfect beings, because that is portrayed in the church.

Let us take a pause for the cause. To all who operate in ministry, please stop painting a picture that just because you have a microphone in your hand or a title before your name, that life in Christianity is perfect. As human beings, everyone is subject to error and sin. It really does vex my spirit when Christians bash others, yet do not take the time to acknowledge their own past and current sins. Yet, they believe that they are going to make it into my kingdom preaching hate theory. Tuh! Unless they repent and truly hear what I am saying to the church, they will have another thing coming on Judgment Day.

As Terrell got dressed for baptism in all white, he was very nervous. He was not sure what would happen nor what this experience would be like for him. One thing that he did expect was that life from this point would be drastically different. Terrell went down to the basement of Temple Revival where his female pastor was waiting for him and the other five individuals that were baptized that day. As he was getting closer to the front, he became even more nervous and anxious. He began to tremble because he just knew that this would be a life-changing experience. He proceeded to step into the cold pool of water. His pastor asked him if he was ready for his life to be changed. With tears in his eyes, he said, "Yes." The pastor, along with two other men, got ready to submerge him into the water.

"I baptize you in the name of the Father, Son, and Holy Spirit," said his pastor with authority. "In Jesus' name, be made whole."

Terrell went down under the water and came back up speaking in tongues, which is one of the gifts and evidence of the Holy Spirit.

As Terrell was worshipping me, my Spirit rested on him heavily. The two men that helped to submerge him had to carry him out of the pool because he was so drunk in the spirit. While he was worshipping, I was able to show him what happened to him in the spirit during the time he was submerged. It seemed like it could have been an illusion. As Terrell was down in the water and being lifted up, the old spirit was released from his body in the water. As Terrell arose anew from the water, the old spirit was reaching for Terrell. When you have been delivered from something, it will always be the desire of the enemy to ensure that there is not a true separation. Terrell got excited that he had become new in my name and identity. This was another level of maturity for him. With every level of maturity, there are lessons that must be learned. He felt as though he could conquer any demon and devil. He also had a friend by the name of Sasha who was very spiritual and liked Terrell. They both liked each other actually, but Terrell was determined not to date Sasha because he still had an attraction to men. He respected their relationship and did not desire to jeopardize it. Terrell came back to school preaching with fire and brimstone. He walked around the hallways and classes quoting scriptures. He would pray for people, as he was led to do by my spirit, and he began to revolutionize the spirit of his classmates. It was refreshing to see someone that was so confused and bitter, become more like me. This was effective until Terrell did what most Christians do, which is become arrogant and condemning.

Let us remember, Terrell had a group of friends that he had befriended that were homosexuals and everyone in the school knew about it. After his baptism, Terrell began to treat his friends as if they were non-existent. He began to shun them and preach at them. When a person walks in the office of the prophet, I show them many things about themselves, others, the earth, and the spirit realm. With that said, Terrell, during his time of prayer and intercession was able to see many things. However, he did not handle well what I had shown him. He would go to certain people and preach to them in a harsh manner about their lives. This began to affect his witness. He was also on the Gospel choir at this time and he felt as though he was the only Holy person in the entire school. Does this person that Terrell had become sound familiar to you at all? The self-righteous, judgmental person who is always throwing the Bible at you? What he did not know was that I had a plan to bring him down from his high horse. No person is to exalt himself or herself higher than I. I am the Lord God, not anyone else.

As Terrell entered into 2006, he became very religious. He was being himself with a mix of everyone else that he saw while being involved in the church scene. He was still talking with Sasha and her family did not like that. Sasha had a cousin named Keisha that Terrell gave a prophetic word to about her life. Keisha was not receptive of the word because it convicted her and she felt as though she was being judged, though she was not. I was just giving her a warning and I had chosen to use Terrell. Keisha would tell Sasha to leave Terrell alone, because he was a faggot, and nothing good would ever come from their relationship. Sasha was also the child of a well-known pastor in the area, but that did not stop Sasha from having feelings for Terrell.

As time continued during March 2006, Terrell preached his first message at Temple Revival on a Friday night. He did very well, even though he was long-winded. This was a great milestone for Terrell because here it is-he is the first male preacher in his family. He had a cousin that he always looked up to who preached as well, and she gave him hope. After he preached the message "God's Got Your Back", he began to become humble. He realized that he could not do this work without my spirit and my guidance.

Being that Terrell was so involved in his church, he was elevated after that sermon to being one of the praise and worship leaders. Along with that, he was appointed, by the leading of me, to have a set of Godparents by the name of Maureen and Marcus Jones. Marcus was one of the sons of the pastor of Temple Revival and Maureen's mother was Terrell's grandmother's best friend. I established this divine connection because I knew that Maureen and Marcus would teach him great lessons. Some of these lessons would be hard, but necessary. We will come back to this a little later in Terrell's story.

As his junior year continued during, Terrell was not just preaching, but he was using his gift of singing. He began to sing in many different places behind many great legends. Due to this, Terrell began again to become a little arrogant and prideful. His friend Shanae from middle school did not even recognize who this new Terrell was.

"Hey T, can I talk to you for a moment?" asked Shanae.

"Of course you can, Shanae!" replied Terrell in a sarcastic tone. "Why would you ask me such an idiotic question? You can talk to me anytime and you should know this."

"I feel like you are trying to play me and everyone else," said Shanae. "You know that I love God. I am finding out about my sexuality as well as being a lesbian, but instead of being my supportive friend, you are becoming a hypocrite."

At this time, Terrell was offended by what Shanae said, and without thinking, he blurted out, "It is not my fault that you are a carpet-munching butch lesbian. You made the choice and I am not affirming of that or you. I know what I did in times past, but that is not who I am anymore."

"How can you say that is not who you are anymore when every time a good-looking dude walks by you, you look him up and down with your mouth open like a dog lapping for water?" Shanae stated, "You have not changed. You have used the Bible and Jesus to try to cover up your attraction. More than that, you have seemed to forget from whence you came, Terrell. You were the one that came out to me just last year. You came to me about Prince and shared all of your sexual stories with me that I did not want to hear. You moved out of your mother's house because she found out that you liked boys. Let us not forget about what you have done, what you are doing currently and what you will do in the future. You have not been delivered Terrell. The church has fooled you and you have been walking around here all year preaching hate to everyone and not being very Christ-like. How can you call yourself a Christian when you do not even show love like God? How can you be a Christian when you are not even being a good fisher of men? Let us not forget, I know that word too. You need to get your shit together. If you were so delivered, you would be with Sasha right now. She loves you and has been waiting on your gay ass since sophomore year. I guess you are too spiritual to see that."

Then she walked away from Terrell. Terrell at this point could not refute what she said. She was one person that actually had the power to shut him up. He could not do anything but stand there and reflect on what she had said. He then went home and reflected on her words. He wondered if those things were the truth or if she was letting the devil use her, so that he would not continue to do what he was led to do. Terrell was not led by me to preach hate to anyone, because I never preached a hate message. Terrell was following what he thought was right based on what the church would say, and most of all he did this to protect his own feelings. Many people use my word as a way to cover their own insecurities.

However, this method is never effective. Feelings, thoughts and emotions are suppressed, but not changed. No matter how much Scripture a person can throw around, it does not mean that they have really changed from the inside. Anyone can change garments, but only I have the ability to change the soul. This was Terrell's wake-up call, letting him know, that what he was doing was incorrect and out of order. I did reprimand him about it as time progressed, and he had to go back and apologize to each person that he criticized, and ostracized in my name. Those previous acts did not bring me glory. He learned the hard way that if you ever exalt yourself higher than others, I always have a way of bringing you back to your state of humility. You will see how this was done in the following chapter.

CHAPTER 6
Do You Love Me?

It was towards the end of Terrell's junior year, and he was having some difficulties deciding exactly what was next for him. As active as he was with the many different activities in school, there was one in particular that Terrell loved. There was a program established by one of the assistant principals at Frank Morrell High called Sons of Promise/Daughters of Destiny. The program was designed to show the young men in this urban community that they were indeed sons of promise and that the females were daughters of destiny. As mentioned previously, Terrell and Sasha were very close and they were both a part of this organization. They would proudly walk the halls of the school and share their stories of how much this program had helped to shape them into the young people that they were. Sasha was currently a senior and Terrell was a junior. He always seemed to like the older crowd.

During the month of April, the Sons of Promise and Daughters of Destiny had a recognition ceremony. The assistant principal had chosen several individuals to speak during the ceremony, and they were given specific words to speak about. Terrell and Sasha were chosen to speak that night. When it was Terrell's turn, I began to work and Terrell was able to minister under the power of the Holy Spirit. Even though this was not a church service, he preached in five minutes and there was a standing ovation. There were many important people in the audience including his family, friends, administration and Sasha's family.

One of Sasha's aunts, Karena, shared with Terrell after he was finished by saying, "While you were ministering, I saw you speaking in front of a large body of people. You have such an anointing on your life and one day you will preach to the masses."

Terrell became overjoyed because he was excited and accepted the prophetic word that had just come to his spirit. He was not excited because his name would be in bright lights, but he was excited because what he spoke into atmospheres shifted the very climate of any room that he was in. It even shifted the atmosphere of the naysayers.

There was one instructor at their high school that Terrell did not like and she did not like him. She had a very evil spirit, but Terrell was not afraid of her. Sasha was in her class for yearbook and her name was Mrs. Bart. Mrs. Bart was short, plump and had an answer for everything. She had known Terrell because he was so involved with everything in school except for her activities. One day, Mrs. Bart spoke with Sasha because she knew that she and Terrell were close.

"Sasha, I am sorry to tell you the news, but you should not expect a future with Terrell," she said while laughing hysterically. "He is clearly a faggot. He does not want what you have and he never will. You might as well just move on,"

This devastated Sasha, even though she already had her suspicions and had been told the same thing. She just believed that if she loved him through his sexual orientation that he would change. Terrell did not feel comfortable speaking with Sasha about this topic. Especially when a person is jealous, they try anything to break up what could be good. Mrs. Bart was not in support of Terrell and did everything that she could to ensure that he and Sasha would not unite.

Along with Mrs. Bart, in this conversation, was Sasha's best friend

Tiffany. Tiffany did not like Terrell because she wanted Sasha to herself. Terrell called this out publicly one day on the third floor as I gave him the revelation, but Sasha did not want to believe it. Sasha then proceeded the next day to tell Terrell what the two of them were saying about him and how they thought this was all a joke.

Terrell said, "As much as I want to curse them out, I will just let God handle them. He always has a way of handling my enemies."

He was very correct in his statement because I honored what Terrell said, especially when it pertained to me. I have told the people not to touch my anointed and do my prophet no harm. Harm is not always physical. It can be emotional, verbal, psychological and spiritual as well. Within the next week from this incident, Sasha came to Terrell in a hurry.

"Terrell!" said Sasha in a frightened tone "Oh my God! What did you do?"

"Oh my God, Sasha," replied Terrell "I didn't do anything. What in the world are you talking about?"

"Mrs. Bart's husband had a heart attack and she also was rushed to the hospital for something severe," replied Sasha. "Tiffany was kicked out of her house and now she has nowhere to live. This is so crazy".

Sasha was very dramatic and ensured that she emphasized every word that came out of her mouth.

"Oh really?" replied Terrell. "My prayer is that they repent and that God has mercy on their souls. I did not do anything. I warned them to keep their mouths off me and they did not listen. Therefore, they will suffer the repercussions."

Sasha looked at Terrell in awe and marveled at the strong man of God that he was even in his youth. She greatly desired to be with him because he reminded her so much of her father who was a bishop.

The struggle between Terrell and Sasha's relationship was obvious. Terrell was more attracted to men than to women. Even in that, he still loved Sasha and wanted to be with her. He did not know how to express himself to her without considering himself as less than a man. This is a common theme amongst men because they do not like to feel less than who they are, especially around a woman. This was a challenge for Terrell and one that he did not know how to handle.

Sasha had a friend by the name of Mike who was a football player. He was a very manly man with muscles. Being that he was an athlete, he felt as though he could do anything or get anyone that he wanted, which was what most athletes that Terrell met did anyway. Mike tried his hardest to ensure that Sasha did not continue to have feelings for Terrell by speaking negatively about him even though he portrayed himself to be Terrell's friend. Terrell was not dumb. He had my spirit and I blessed him with the ability to hear what others who meant him no good.

As junior year was ending, Terrell was asked to go the senior prom with another friend of his named Sharease who was on the Gospel choir at Frank Morrell. He had known Sharease and her twin since middle school and knew that they would have a good time. Terrell was dressed in his white and peach along with Sharease. They complemented each other well, but Terrell wanted to go to the prom with Sasha. She did not even accept his offer to go to prom because she was not sure if she was going to attend.

Once they arrived at the venue, Terrell saw many of his friends. The most elegant person that he saw that night was Sasha who was wearing lavender. Terrell spent most of the prom with Sasha and he thought that they would be a couple in the very near future. While there, Mike saw that Sasha and Terrell were together. He decided to come over and grab Sasha to make her dance. Terrell allowed him to have his little fun because he knew that Sasha did not like Mike in that way based on what she had shared with him. Little did Terrell know Sasha was lying to him.

The school year had ended and Terrell was trying to figure out what was in store for him during his senior year. He could not believe that he had made it this far, but he did with my assistance. Everything seemed to be going well until he received a phone call that shook his very core.

"Terrell, I am just so upset," said Sasha.

"Well, why are you upset?" said Terrell with compassion. "You just graduated and had a great prom. You are legal to do what you want with the approval of your father. There is so much to be happy about."

"Well, I am still upset," said Sasha "I don't like for people to play games with me and my emotions.

"What in the world are you talking about Sasha?" replied Terrell in a confused tone.

"I am talking about Mike," Sasha said with disgust. "He is such a jerk. We went out on a date the other night to the movies and I saw his ex-girlfriend there. After he pretended as though we were not dating, he wanted to have sex with me in the theater to make her jealous. I just do not like when boys try to use me. I am a good girl."

As Terrell was hearing this information, he was crushed. He had never known that Sasha and Mike were actually dating. This was not information that she had shared in times past.

"So you mean to tell me that you are dating Mike?" said Terrell angrily. "The one that does not like me! The one that you told me you did not have feelings for? The one that I told you would be using you anyway.

Really, Sasha? How in the hell could you lie to me about this?"

"Well Terrell, I did not feel like I owed you any explanation because we were not dating," replied Sasha "What would be the point of me telling you that I have been dating someone for the past 5 months? If you wanted to know, you should have asked and you should have been paying attention. It was very obvious."

"You want to know what is obvious, Sasha?" Terrell said. "I will tell you. You are such a spoiled bitch. The only reason why you decided to tell me that you were dating Mike was because he made you mad. If he did not make you upset, you still would not have told me. I trusted you. I believed in you. I believed in US. I love you, Sasha. Yet, you played with my heart and my emotions. You did not really want me as much as you claim that you did. If so, we would not be having this conversation. You know what, though? I am done. I am done with you and I am done with females.

"You know how I felt about the last girl that I dated and what she did to me. I feel like you have done the exact same thing. You decided to date a more masculine person who was an athlete. Mike is dumb as shit. He never goes to class and he is always talking about how much pussy he gets. With all of the alleged common sense, where was yours? You could not see that this athlete was trying to fuck the preacher's daughter? You are actually dumber than I thought. You can keep Mike. Keep your relationship and leave me alone. I actually brought you around my family and this is how you repay me? Bye, Sasha."

This was the final conversation that Terrell had with Sasha. Both of them were devastated and emotional. For Terrell, this was the end. He was more hurt because he thought that Sasha was different. He thought that she would have been the one, but instead, she was the one to hurt him the most.

From this point on, Terrell lost his faith because what he loved again did not love him. This caused him to retract back into his old ways because he figured that he would never make it with a female.

I am sure that as you are reading this you can understand what Terrell was feeling. Unbelievably, many people still feel this exact way, but suppress it. Terrell tried to suppress it as much as he could, but there was no holding back this monster. He felt helpless, hopeless, and out of control. What he did not understand was that he was never in control. I am always in control and I have the master plan. This was just the beginning of his time of trial and error.

CHAPTER 7
Crazy in Love

During the summer leading into his senior year, Terrell was still very confused. He was not sure how he missed the deception of Sasha, and was not a fan of being a marriage counselor to his parents. It is surely a difficult situation when parents are married and they express their issues to their children. Yes, it is good to be transparent and honest, but kids need to be kids. Teenagers have their own problems and identities to deal with. It becomes much more stressful for the teenager when they have to keep peace in a home full of chaos. Even in the chaos, Terrell found a sense of solitude.

He was still singing with the Gospel groups and trying to suppress his feelings. He wanted love. He wanted to be cared for genuinely, but did not know what true love meant or felt like. He thought throughout his life at this point that people showed their love towards him by abusing him or using him for what he had to offer. During the summer of 2006 when MySpace was famous, Terrell received a message in his inbox from this boy that he had been seeing at church. I was telling Terrell not to get involved in this relationship, but one thing about him is that when he likes someone, he will disobey me to fill the void of love in his life. They never really spoke in person, but always linked eyes. Terrell always had a weakness for light skin. The boy was Rommell McAdams, the apple of Terrell's eye. From their initial conversation on MySpace, they exchanged numbers and talked every day for hours. After talking and sharing intimate details about one another, they became a couple in a matter of days. They both loved each other and this was so different for Rommell.

Rommell had just graduated from high school in Newark, NJ and was about to start college in the fall. He always had the dream to work in the media, which Terrell admired. Now, as high maintenance as Terrell was, Rommell was very different. He lived in the projects and was adopted. Since Terrell was only 16 at the time, he was not able to drive without an adult. Therefore, he would take the bus to go and see Rommell. This was also Rommell's first relationship with a male. Here we have Terrell who is already experienced and has a strong idea of what he does not want to repeat from Prince and O'Neil. With this in mind, two weeks into their relationship, a problem occurred. See, Rommell was still dealing with his ex-girlfriend named Nashanna. Terrell did not know that they were still messing around because Rommell did not tell him until after he cheated with her.

"Yo, T!" said Rommell. "I am so sorry. I did not mean to cheat on you. I really do love you. This is just hard. I do not know how to deal with being with another dude. I have never done this and I am scared. I need you to forgive me, though. Please don't leave me so soon."

"I am not going to leave you," replied Terrell. "But you have to promise me that you won't do anything like that again. I already have trust issues and this is not helping at all." From that point forward, even though Terrell loved Rommell, he really did not trust him. He always thought in the back of his mind that Rommell would cheat on him again, just like Toya, Prince and Sasha had. With these thoughts, Terrell began to become crazy in love...literally.

In September of 2006, Terrell turned 17. He was so excited about his birthday because he was going to spend it with Rommell and family. On this same day, he went to take his test to obtain his driver's license. He was very afraid because he did not want to fail this test. He could not wait to drive on his own because when his parents were in the car with him, they always had something to say. Don't you hate when people are riding with you and they are trying to tell you how to drive? This is the same way that Terrell felt, which inspired him to obtain his license at 17. Upon entering the DMV and the teacher coming out, Terrell did not know what to expect. When the teacher entered the car, he did not greet Terrell. Instead, he told Terrell to follow the directions that he gave, which Terrell did. When the driving test was over, the man got out of the car and told Terrell, "You passed. Come and get your license".

Terrell could not believe that he had finally gotten his license. He felt like he was on top of the world. After his license was printed, he called his mother to tell her and she was proud. Things at this point seemed to be going well for Terrell, but there was a side of him that had yet to be revealed.

With the events that transpired with Terrell in the past with infidelity and non-commitment from his ex-lovers, Terrell became infatuated with another young man who attended some of the same church functions as he did named Peanut. Peanut would hang with these other people named Steele, Leshawn, and Dana. Terrell being young and naïve also began to hang with this group of people without thinking much of it. Terrell was always a hot commodity. Being young, intelligent and good-looking was something that always intrigued both males and females. Terrell and Peanut exchanged numbers and became good friends. Peanut was shorter than Terrell, but Terrell loved his smile as well as his intellect. Not to mention, in Terrell's eyes, Peanut had a lot more to offer being that he was older and independent. One night, Terrell decided to leave his parent's house and go spend some time with Peanut. After about two hours of conversing and watching movies,

Peanut pulled out his penis. In Terrell's mind, he was saying to himself, "Lord, HELP".

Then Peanut motioned for him to give him a kiss and Terrell submitted. Do not judge Terrell. Your flesh I am sure has been out of control as well. It happens. I told Terrell not to get involved sexually because there is a transfer of spirits that happens when people are involved intimately. Some people wonder why they are different after intercourse and it is because they did not know the spirit that was operating in the person that they opened themselves up to. Anyways, Terrell ended up having sex with Peanut and to him, it was amazing. Even in the amazement, Terrell had now cheated on Rommell. Here is when everything began to go downhill in their relationship.

As time progressed, Terrell began to want Peanut more than he wanted Rommell. At this point, because Terrell was infatuated with Peanut, he did not want Rommell to know anything at all about their encounter. He felt that Rommell would dump him if he told him.

Terrell suffered from something that many people suffer from, which is abandonment. In his past, he was abandoned and felt as though the only way he could be loved was by abuse. His relationship with Rommell began to become very strained. In October of that same year, Terrell was so paranoid that Rommell was cheating that he began to become very demanding and selfish.

Terrell would make requests to have every password to everything that Rommell had. He began to check Rommell's phone logs, texts, social media and anything else just to prove to himself that Rommell was cheating. His logic was that, "I already believe that he is doing it, so why not? I can hurt him before he hurts me again".

As some of you are reading this, I am sure that you are seeing yourself in Terrell. Because you felt like you would lose something or someone, you began to become controlling. Being a controlling person does not cause love to grow stronger, but instead has the ability to cause the relationship to end.

Terrell became so compulsive and obsessed that it affected his state of mind and his spirit. Instead of me being his God, Rommell became his God. He was the one that Terrell worshipped and spent the most time with. He did not spend as much time with me and neglected our relationship. I am a very jealous God. For my own creation to worship someone else is not acceptable to me at all. I was trying to get his attention, but he was not listening. Therefore, I decided to withdraw my spirit from him. He would lead praise and worship at his church and there would be no anointing. The anointing is not something that is given freely and if I have instructed a person to do something and they disobey, then they sacrifice what I have given them. You must pay for the anointing and live a life that I am pleased with, but because Terrell was, deliberately doing what he thought was right even though I told him it was wrong, I removed my spirit from him.

One Sunday, Terrell brought Rommell to church when he was leading praise and worship.

At that time, Terrell's Godfather Marcus said to him after praise and worship, "Who is that fag that you brought with you to church? God is not going to honor that and you must get right now."

Even though I understand where Marcus was coming from, I never tell people to condemn and bash a person no matter who they are. I love everyone and show him or her love. How can a person be delivered if there is no love shown and their approach is offensive instead of helpful? My point is that it will not work out well. Marcus was wrong for calling the young man that name. I do not see him as a faggot nor do I address him as such.

Terrell replied to Marcus, "Don't call him that name because you don't even know him so why are you saying something so evil? Man! Whatever, get out my face."

He then walked off in anger out of the sanctuary. He did not understand why a child of mine who did not understand a struggle would be so judgmental. All along, Terrell had been attending this church and no one had ever had a conversation about his life. His Godfather honestly did not know how to handle a situation of this sort because he had never dealt with it from anyone else. Which brings me to another point: When you do not understand something, ASK! There are too many hurt people in the world. They come to my house for refuge, yet they leave heavier than when they entered. It is not your job to judge, it is mine.

Terrell began to distance himself from his Godfather from that day forward since he was homophobic. Terrell did not talk with his Godfather for a long time. His Godfather was a Christian and he thought that he would have more compassion, but what Terrell learned was that if someone has not dealt with an experience firsthand, then they will not know how to handle the situation nor those people who are involved in that situation.

As time continued to progress, Terrell and Peanut were still having seeing each other until Terrell realized something after a conversation they had.

"Hey Peanut, would you be in a relationship with me?" asked Terrell.

"Yes, I would, but you are so young," replied Peanut. "You are only 17 and I am 24. You still have a lot to learn and I don't want to hinder your growth process."

"Oh! So I am too young for you to date, but I am not too young for you to fuck, huh?" replied Terrell in an angry tone.

This became a very heated discussion, which caused Terrell to learn that he was being used. He realized that who he wanted, did not want him in the same regard and used age as an excuse. With this situation going on and not talking with anyone about it, Terrell became more hostile with Rommell.

In December 2006, Terrell began working in retail at Ralph Lauren in Short Hills Mall. He had his license and he loved the brand. He felt as though the manager of the store was attracted to him, but was not going to cross those lines. During the time that he was working at Ralph Lauren, he also applied for a job to work at Old Navy in Newark, which was not too far from his house. The main motivation for him desiring to work at Old Navy was to be closer to Rommell. Once Terrell got the job at Old Navy, Rommell was not happy. He felt as though Terrell was smothering him and complained about everything. This was all a part of the insecurity that Terrell possessed.

In January 2007, Terrell was preparing to celebrate Rommell's birthday. He made plans and wanted to do something great to make his boyfriend happy. With these plans in mind, the demons that were in Terrell did not allow him to have a happy night. That evening of the 14th, Terrell and Rommell went out. Things were going well until Terrell's guilt and insecurity began to show. They began arguing in the car in the darkness of the night. While they were around the corner from Rommell's project apartment complex, Terrell told Rommell, "Get the hell out of my car then if you don't like the way that I am".

While he was saying this statement, he pushed Rommell out of his car and proceeded to drive off.

As he was heading down the road, he realized that he was out of control and backed the car to where Rommell was. He was trying to get his attention, but Rommell was ignoring him and crying. The look on his face was that of disgust and hurt because he did not know why his boyfriend would do that to him. Rommell did get back into the car because it was raining outside. Terrell was very apologetic, but Rommell was through with Terrell. The next day Rommell broke up with him. Terrell was in disbelief and did not want to accept the fact that he had been dumped. The hurt of losing his love caused him to become even more obsessed with Rommell.

Even though Terrell and Rommell did break up, that was not the end of the rage of Terrell. He was literally crazy in love with Rommell. However, Rommell was the only person that Terrell really did love with all his heart. It was very hard for him to get over Rommell because they did so much together, but I caused this to end for a reason. Terrell was aware that Rommell began seeing another person named Darryl. Even though Terrell and Rommell were not together, they were still having sex. On several occasions, Terrell dropped Rommell off at Darryl's house and never knew they were dating until later on. This caused Terrell to be furious. He would ride by Darryl's house as well as Rommell's multiple times of the day as well as in the evening. He would sit up the street and call Rommell to get no answer. Terrell was really becoming insane if I can say so myself.

After Rommell and Darryl ended, Rommell began to see Steele, who was one of Peanut's close friends. This made Terrell furious because Steele was also trying to sleep with him while he knew that he was dating Rommell. Steele was always a messy spirited person. He would play in church all the time and he knew that he was too old to be doing that. Terrell and Steele really parted ways when Terrell made the decision to be friends with Leshawn. This upset Steele, but Terrell was glad that he made that decision. Leshawn was the one that helped Terrell dress couture for his high school senior prom and many other things. Terrell felt as though Steele and Rommelle's way to get back at him was to date each other.

Through all of this, Terrell became very bitter and people did not want to be around him because of how mean he had become. The majority of the people that had shown their love to him were not talking to him anymore because his attitude became such a turn off. The only thing that Terrell had to do was learn to communicate.

One Sunday, Terrell had on a wristband that stated, "Noah's Arc". The writing was black and a person could not really see the words unless they were paying attention. When people at his church asked him what the arc meant in comparison to the ark in the Bible, Terrell would lie. Noah's Arc was a show that came on LOGO, which depicted the lives of gay African-American men. There was also a show called "Queer as Folk" that Terrell used to watch during his earlier days of high school, but he never spoke about it. One day, his Godfather Marcus, told him that he knew what Noah's Arc meant. He then asked Terrell if he knew what the real meaning was and again Terrell lied. Even though Terrell did not care for his Godfather due to him being offended, he very much feared and respected him.

Once his Godfather confronted him, Terrell discarded the bracelet and continued to watch the show in secret. Isn't that sad? Youth cannot seem to be honest with adults because they fear that they will be judged and ostracized. After realizing that his life was going downward, he decided to come back to me. I was there waiting for him to realize that he would need to submit to my will again and it felt great to have him back.

Terrell began to do my will during the end of his senior year and his life changed drastically. He began walking more in his calling of being a prophet, evangelist, and teacher. He learned that in his life, I am the one who is able to justify the person I called and/or am well pleased. He was one of those people who pleased my heart because he was now more aware than he was before. He saved the Gospel Choir from being removed from the high school amongst many other things in my name, and the only thing that people could say about him was that he was a homosexual. There was nothing else to be said that could degrade his character. I allowed all of this stuff to happen to him because I knew that he would not curse me and die. I knew that all of this would build him up as a person and a great leader.

Therefore, Terrell, I speak to you again and give you a command. "You will lift up your eyes unto the hills, from whence cometh your help. Your help cometh from ME, which made heaven and earth. I will not suffer thy foot to be moved: I that keepeth YOU will not slumber. Behold, I that keepeth Israel shall neither slumber nor sleep. I AM YOUR keeper: I AM thy shade upon thy right hand. The sun shall not smite YOU by day, or the moon by night. I shall preserve YOU from all evil: I shall preserve YOUR soul. I shall preserve YOUR going out and YOUR coming in from this time forth, and even for evermore."

After hearing me speak, Terrell was able to minister at his high school graduation. After all that he endured, he graduated in the top 7% of his class with honors. He led a song called "I Believe" by Fantasia. I promise you, while he was singing, I came down into that arena and I showed up and showed out. The preacher that was in Terrell surely manifested and my spirit moved so that people were able to be encouraged and uplifted. All because he had my spirit despite his struggle.

CHAPTER 8
Wake-Up Call

After graduation from high school, Terrell was still not clear as to what he was going to do with his life. He was living with his parents and his life seemed to be a bit chaotic. By this time, he was still not sure about his previous relationship with Rommell, but he also knew that he would need to leave his comfort zone. He had been in New Jersey for 17 years and it was time for something different. Just as many of you who are reading this can attest, just because you are comfortable in a place does not mean that it is meant for you to reside there for the rest of your life. Terrell was enjoying his time in NJ during the month of June, and he met someone else in the church circuit that he had no idea he would fall for.

There was this short man by the name of Quinton Edwards who had had his eye on Terrell for a long time, but who had never approached him until one day, while at IHOP. Terrell always played hard to get because he was not like the other loose individuals that he had met in the church circuit. What started as an initial conversation grew into a relationship fast. Quinton was also a very spiritual person and he was 12 years older than Terrell. As the summer, days went on, Terrell and Quinton became close to the point that Terrell's mother even knew who Quinton was. Even though at this point, Terrell never had that conversation with his mother, she knew what was going on, but did not want to believe it. We will revisit this later along Terrell's journey.

Terrell and Quentin were now involved in a relationship and were having intercourse unprotected. Terrell did not really pay attention in sex education class while in high school and no one in the family spoke about the dangers of having sex unprotected. In fact, Terrell did not have protected sex because he felt as though there was nothing that could ever happen to him. I find this to be funny about most people, because they believe that they are exempt from things in life, because they have a relationship with me, when that is not always factual.

One day, while Terrell was sitting in his room, he began to wonder about college and figured that he would just go to Essex County College for two years free, and transfer to Rutgers University. He had applied to other colleges in NJ as well as other places, being that he had gone on the Black College Tours that Ms. Lane, Mrs. Oglesby, and Mr. Bragg had taken students on in the spring semester. During the spring of 2007, they visited a college in South Carolina called Confidence University. While visiting CU, Terrell was able to audition with the music department because he wanted to teach music at his high school after college graduation. He met with the music faculty and they really did enjoy him. There was a young woman by the name of Jennifer who really worked with Terrell during his admissions process and he was accepted into the school.

While this was a joy for Terrell, it was also very challenging. Growing up in a single parent home with low-income, Terrell did not have the chance to travel much. He knew about South Carolina because his mother and grandmother were from that state, but Terrell did not want to go that far because he was afraid. One day, during the summer of 2007 as Terrell was watching cartoons, I spoke to him with a loud voice and said, "If you do not leave this place, you shall surely die." I remember him telling me years ago, "Lord, I don't ever want to move down south. Those people are country and I just do not want to move there. It's too hot and I don't like being in heat."

I laughed at Terrell. He is such a dramatic person sometimes, but I find it hysterical that he would tell me where he was not going to go. Jonah also told me that he was not going where I sent him, and you see that I sent a fish to consume him and place him right where I told him to go. One way or another, Terrell was going, because I had need of him in South Carolina. He was going to grow so much under the new ministry, new atmosphere, and new people and make a difference in the city.

When Terrell heard me speak, he did not hesitate to tell his parents that same day that he had to go to college in SC. Of course, being that he was a momma's boy, she was supportive, but did not want to see her baby boy go. Many people did not understand this, but this was all part of the Jeremiah anointing that I placed on his life. When I tell him to go, he must go where I say go and speak what I say speak. From that day in the middle of July, Terrell had to figure out what the next steps were for him. He had a "Going Away" service at his home church and at another church because he wanted everyone to feel welcomed. He was excited about going away, but was not sure of how this new relationship with Quinton would work. I do have a way of getting people to leave their familiar place so that I can mold them into who I have called them to be. I am grateful that Terrell chose to be obedient during this time and make the necessary sacrifices so that he could live.

One Sunday afternoon, Terrell and Quinton were in a service and Rommelle came in with Steele. Even though by this time, Rommelle and Terrell had not been together since January and it was now late July, they still had feelings for each other. The service went very high in my name, but then something happened. As church was dismissing, Rommell was running to the back gasping for air. When Terrell saw this, he immediately went running to the back and picked Rommelle up to carry him outside.

"Someone call the ambulance!" Terrell shouted. "He is having an asthma attack. Someone call Big Mac! She needs to know what is going on."

As people were standing around looking, he saw Steele come out of the church and came alongside Rommelle.

As Steele was transferring Rommelle to the hospital, Terrell took Quinton's car to go and alert Big Mac. Quinton was hurt because he saw the urgency that Terrell had for Rommelle, but he understood that he could not compete with history. Once Terrell alerted Big Mac, a group of people, including Quinton, went to the hospital to see about Rommelle. He was hooked to machines and had a breathing mask on. Even though he could not speak, he did get a piece of paper to communicate with Terrell when Steele and the others were not around. The note said, "Thank you for saving me. I really do appreciate it and I love you." Terrell did not do anything but nod his head and smile. Steele was upset, but Terrell did not care at all. He left the hospital feeling as though this was the start of a new beginning in his life. He thought about if he and Rommelle would reconnect, but I had to remind him that I had called him to go somewhere else to do a new work.

August 2007 has come and Terrell is departing for college. What an exciting time for him and his family! Eyes have not seen, nor did ears hear, neither had it entered into the heart of man the great things that I had in store for Terrell. I was so excited for him. I was even more amazed that his life was one that I put together. I said to myself, "You are great and mighty." and I replied to myself and said, "I know", while laughing hysterically.

He was the first one to go off to college out of his family and he did not know what to expect. Over 700 miles away from home in Orangeburg, SC is where I had to send Terrell, and he had no idea what was awaiting him at CU.

This journey ended with him leaving his family and friends up north and traveling across the country to the South, to be in a land that was strange to him, but he had an assignment.

"Oh my God!" said Terrell. It is so hot down here." "Lord! Why in the world would you send me to a place that you know I do not want to be in? It is all right, though. I am here and I will do what you have told me. You know me and my life better than I do."

Hundreds of people were there, both students and their families, along with the school faculty.

"Oh so they put me in this dorm of 6 floors with one elevator." He said this aloud and people were looking at him as though they knew whom not to mess with at this school. "What the hell? How do they expect all these boys to move into this dorm and it is hot as hell out here with that one elevator? See, this is what I am talking about!"

As Terrell walked through CU, he noted that many people would just look at him and speak. Now common courtesy would be to speak back, but at that time, if Terrell did not know a person, he would not speak. Being from Newark, NJ it was not common to just pass by and speak especially considering the fact that Terrell was from the ghetto. However, as time progressed, Terrell began to loosen up and talk to more people, but he was very cautious. I gave him the gift of discernment so he could see into a person's spirit, which allowed him to know who to connect with and who not to.

During this first orientation week at CU, Terrell met many people from the President on down to the janitorial staff. One night, I remember he was at a retreat with his fellow classmates, after his mother and father had already traveled back to the North. He was sitting on a hill with a girl named Michelle that he found very attractive and some other firsttime freshman.

Moreover, I was the topic of the discussion. They noticed that Terrell was a prophet because what he spoke about was so accurate pertaining to their lives and when he spoke, there was such authority and power. What they did not know however was his multiple struggles. There are things that are better left unsaid.

The first semester at CU was not hard for Terrell at all. He has always been able to adapt to new places easily. He became the leader of the freshman Gospel choir called "Good News," president of his dorm council, and Mr. Freshman just to name a few of his accomplishments. Even though Terrell was very involved upon moving to this new place, he still had much maturing to do. Along with trying to understand his sexuality, he was still very rude and had no tact when talking to people. Yes, Terrell did have to speak what I told him to speak, but there are still ways to say things to people. Terrell did not care who you were as a person. If he had something to say, he would and whichever way it came out is how he meant it, which turned people off from him. This was a humbling experience for Terrell because those that he needed to help bring his vision to pass were leaving him due to his lack of compassion.

Another thing that helped him to be humble and grow in the anointing that I placed on him was Praise of Life Ministries. Terrell was led to visit Praise of Life after he had heard the name of the ministry. He visited the ministry twice before joining by my leading, which surely carried him through his transition from NJ to SC. I must say that I was happy with Terrell. While attending this new church, he began to grow and really was on fire for me. The people on the campus knew him as "The rude well dressed boy that loves Jesus, sings, and is a prophet." He had some trouble adjusting because the town that his college was in was very desolate. Terrell was from a big city where there were buses, trains, taxicabs and many stores. In Orangeburg at the time, they did not even have a bus. The people in the town hung out at WalMart or at their respective churches. In order to get around, a person had to walk or drive. This was very different for Terrell, but it allowed him the opportunity to grow and develop.

While attending CU during the first semester, Terrell acquired many acquaintances and as time progressed, he began to see the true colors of many individuals. This caused him to limit those he called friend.

He majored in music and spent most of his time practicing classical music, and in his spare time, he went to church. Of his friends, (there was one young man that I gave him specific instructions for), named D'Angelo, was similar to Terrell, but his attitude and disposition were worse. He was a transfer student who thought that the he was on top of the world and everyone else was a peasant.

I told Terrell the following: "D'Angelo needs help with finding himself spiritually and he needs to be introduced to me in a new way. You are to befriend him and work through the walls that he has up so that the essence of who he is can be manifested. This is an assignment from me and you are only to do as I have instructed you to do." Terrell heard what I spoke unto him and he obeyed for the most part.

During his first semester, he and Quinton were still conversing, but they were not dating. During their conversations, they were sharing with one another how they had not been with anyone else since their last encounter during the latter part of July. Terrell believed that they were doing a good job with their discipline. While being in college during the first semester, he did not have any sexual encounters with any males until Herbert came along. Herbert was a masculine person that had a swag that caught Terrell's attention. Terrell was attracted to his bright smile and personality. During the later portion of the semester right before Thanksgiving, Terrell had two encounters with Herbert. Even though they did not have full intercourse, Terrell believed that Herbert was a possible relationship item. One night while visiting another campus with some of his friends Damone, Arthur & Herman, he found out something different. Terrell discovered after speaking with his friends, that Herbert was trying to have an encounter with not just his friends, but was actually the campus whore. This devastated Terrell because he did not know why he had to be the guinea pig, but he was grateful that at least it had happened to him and not to his friends.

Once Terrell considered someone a friend, he really did care about him or her. His friends actually became like his family. One thing about family is that it is not always about genetics, but it is about those who you can trust as well as call on during different times in your life. As that night ended and they returned to the dormitory, Terrell began to question himself and blame himself for even having an encounter with a person like Herbert.

"How could I not see this?" Terrell said to me during his time of meditation. "How did I not know? This is horrible. I should have just remained to myself, but it is what it is. The semester is over and 2008 will be here. This is just a lesson learned. Just because a person has, swag does not mean that they are meant to be pursued beyond what they really want, which is sex. At least I did not have a full encounter with him. Lord, you only know what he has going on. Thank you for that protection."

I protected him then, and I always will. Contrary to popular belief, I am always with you. I even said it in my word that I will be with you always, even until the ends of the earth.

During December of 2007, Terrell finished the semester strong with a 3.5 GPA and came back up north to visit his family for the extended break. He was excited to be home and possibly rekindling his flame with Quinton, the young man he was involved with during the summer. In January of 2008, a week before Terrell was going back down to CU, Quinton and Terrell were together, and one thing was leading to another. They began to kiss, and clothes came off. Please do not act as though this is a surprise while you are reading it. For those of you who have been in situations such as Terrell, you know what happens when clothes come off. While they were getting ready to engage in sexual intercourse as Terrell was lying there, I spoke and the words I gave him to speak at that time were, "And do this in remembrance of me".

Terrell covered his mouth after I spoke through him and Quinton put his head down because he knew me as well. Terrell and Quinton just began to laugh.

"Well the Lord stopped this for some reason or another," said Terrell. "That has never happened. Here the word of God comes right out of my mouth to stop me from committing an act. Thank you, Lord."

Terrell got dressed, packed up his things and proceeded to go home. On Thursday of that same week, Terrell got a call from a mutual friend saying that Quinton was having flu like symptoms. Terrell went over to the house the next day and took Quinton to his doctor's appointment. They sat in the waiting room and I told Terrell that when Quinton was called in to go into the room with him to see the doctor. He did not know why I was doing this, but he went. As he was sitting there playing his video game, he was asking me why I had him come there.

As the doctor came in and greeted them, he began to review Quinton's chart on the computer.

"Mr. Quinton, Have you been drinking any fluids?" he said.

"Yes, sir," replied Quinton. "I just have not had that much food to eat because I am on a consecration for the month of January."

"Well, you must drink plenty of water to stay hydrated because you are HIV positive, so you have to stay healthy to keep your viral loads down."

When the doctor said those words "HIV positive, Quinton sat up on the doctor's table and Terrell froze playing his game, wondering if he had contracted the disease as well.

"I did not know that I was HIV positive," said Quinton with tears in his eyes "No one ever told me."

"Well, we sent out paper work at the end of November when you came in for blood work," replied the doctor. "I thought that you would have received it. I am sorry for breaking the news to you like this!" T h e room became silent and Terrell was praying to me again, but he was also furious with Quinton. As they walked out of the doctor's office, Terrell said nothing to Quinton until he spoke to him.

"Baby, I am sorry," Quinton said. I did not know that I had this. You still love me, don't you?"

"I need to find a clinic and get tested now," Terrell replied angrily and concerned "I cannot have this disease! I do not believe you! You have been having sex with guys while I was at school and you did not even tell me. You put my life at risk so that you could get a nut. I do not believe this. I do not have anything to say to you. Where is a clinic that I go can go and get tested right now?"

The entire ride to a nearby clinic Terrell was as quiet as the ocean at night. He was worried about his health and was just praying that he did not contact the disease.

"Lord, I am too young to have HIV," he said to me. "I did not even know that he had it. I have never been with someone who has HIV. I have ministry to do and a life to live. What will my mother say? What will my family say? This is so embarrassing. I am so out of sorts right now. Jesus help me please,"

Terrell was tested and his results came back negative. Once Quinton was informed that Terrell was negative, he then told Terrell the truth.

"Terrell, while you were away, I lied to you," he confessed. I actually had unprotected sex with three different guys from August until December. I didn't think that this was going to happen to me and I am sorry for putting you in danger and not informing you about the truth."

"I don't want to have anything to do with you," replied Terrell "I cannot even forgive you right now. I thank God that his Word is in me because if I would have had sex with you, I would be positive right now. I do not ever want to talk to you again, you damn liar. If I was positive, I swear to you, I would have killed you. I would not have thought twice about it, but your life would have been over. Goodbye sir." Then he slammed the phone down.

I spared his life and most of all; he had my Word in his heart that he would not sin against me. I was able to impart in him life and now he can live life more abundantly. Granted everyone makes mistakes in life and will sin, as humans are born into a sinful nature. However, there is sin that can be avoided simply by making a conscious choice followed by discipline.

While in college during his second semester, Terrell was able to minister to so many since that health scare that he had. He was able to minister to the young men about many different things. He was able to use his struggle as a tool to minister to those who had similar experiences. Yes, people did not agree with his lifestyle, but he was working to help save souls that they might come into my kingdom so that I could heal them and set them free. He was doing something that most Christians do not; evangelize-going out to those whom others were afraid to talk to, and ministering to them.

Later that spring, the young man D'Angelo, whom Terrell had known since coming into the university, began to gravitate more to him. As stated before in this chapter, I told Terrell to minister to D'Angelo and that was all. Terrell, as Joshua in the Bible, had the ability to break down the walls that normal people could not break. Therefore, Terrell did as he was instructed and D'Angelo began to know me more in depth. He started attending church with Terrell, Michelle, Marie and Queen. However, again Terrell did not follow my instructions wholeheartedly.

I once was flesh so I understand what it feels like to be attracted to someone else. I really do because I was tempted on all sides yet I never sinned. Not saying that Terrell could do that because he is not me, but he did not follow what I said. Terrell and D'Angelo began to have feelings for one another. People should not mix ministry and relationships together because they will not work out! Terrell knew that he was wrong for engaging with D'Angelo on a relationship level. He was convicted by what he was doing that he stopped going to church because he was afraid that I would expose him.

Eventually, Terrell came back to the church I called him to, and I did just as he feared. I used the Pastor of that church to speak into his life and bring him back to a place of submission because he knew he was doing wrong and I was not going to allow that. I did not allow the situation at hand to be exposed, but there was an exposure to his disobedience. Sometimes it takes a public word for people to understand that I am omnipresent. No one can run from me. Ask Adam and Eve.

"Lord, I am sorry!" Terrell cried. "I should have listened to you. Please forgive me and I will stop this. I promise."

I honored his request and Terrell ended that relationship with D'Angelo, but still wanted to remain friends. One thing about Terrell is that he cannot run for long. I always have a way of getting him back into his rightful place. He brings a lot of judgment from me on himself because he thinks that I will compromise and smile on his disobedience and I will not. He will just suffer if he chooses to disobey, as will others. Some say that is mean, but it is not. All that I do is right and good. It all has a purpose. Just because it is not understood does not mean that it does not have a purpose. I do not reveal all of my secrets at one time because then the people will miss the process of getting to know me in the fullness of who I am. The process of life is necessary. This experience was necessary and humbling. He realized that he could not lead the Gospel choir when he was doing the same as the president before him. There was no way that an excuse could be made. I do not have respect of persons. Judgment is judgment.

Since Terrell had learned that lesson, he and D'Angelo were still friends and freshman year had ended. Many had come and more had left Terrell's life because I did not need him around many people who had motives of corrupting him.

During the summer of 2008, I blessed Terrell while back home up north with his very own vehicle. With that, he was able to come back down for school in the fall. During that time, he engaged in another relationship with an older man by the name of Anthony. It was amazing how Anthony and Terrell were acquainted, but they had a little summer fling. Terrell did not like to be by himself. This is another problem with the fatherless son. Many times, the males look for people to fill the void and want to be loved. They do not know how to properly express themselves without giving themselves to others. Terrell had this problem because he never felt whole unless he was in a relationship with someone else.

Anthony also had a girlfriend and Terrell was not pleased with the fact that Anthony was having sex with him and her. Every time Terrell brought up this subject, Anthony got upset. Terrell did not stress about it too much because Anthony treated him well. Even though this relationship had the potential to keep Terrell from returning to SC where I called him, he knew that if he stayed in Jersey, he would surely die. He remembered what I spoke to him and made his way back down to SC where another journey awaited him.

CHAPTER 9
Who's the Joke Now?

As Terrell's sophomore year of college was starting, he went back down to CU early because he was now an orientation leader. He was responsible for a number of new freshmen to ensure that they were acclimated to CU, as he had been the previous summer. Terrell was very excited to serve and he was a natural leader. There was so much untapped potential in him and using him in these outlets helped him to develop into who he is today.

As orientation was approaching, he was working very closely with the Freshman College under the direction of Ms. Lyles and the other FC staff. Just the year prior, neither Ms. Lyles nor her staff liked Terrell because he was very bossy. However, in a year's time, I changed him because he was willing to be changed.

During his time of being an orientation leader, he met some great freshman students that he befriended and provided words of wisdom.. He was called an old man because Terrell never acted his age. He is wise far beyond his years and does not do all of the normal things that most young people do and that is because I called him to be different.

There was a young man that Terrell met during his first year through a mutual friend named Molstelar. Molstelar had a serious crush on Terrell, but nothing ever happened between them because Terrell did not believe in having encounters or dating a friend's ex. Molstelar moved into the dorm on campus and along came a roommate that caught Terrell's attention. His name was Lavorian. Now, Lavorian was not Terrell's typical type being that he was dark-skinned, short and slim, but they connected somehow and began to get to know each other. During this time, Terrell was living on campus and had two roommates. One was Mark and the other was his ex, D'Angelo. D'Angelo and Terrell had already arranged to stay in the same room during their first year, but with the turn of events that had happened; he was not sure how this would turn out.

At this time, Terrell was still a music major and so was Lavorian. This caused them to spend a lot of time together with long practices and traveling with the concert choir. Over time, Terrell became like family to Lavorian's family, which he liked. He did not like, however, the way his relationship was with D'Angelo. As D'Angelo began to see that Terrell was dating someone else, this caused him to be enraged. There were many days, living in a three-person room that D'Angelo did not speak to Terrell. This caused such friction in their relationship that their once close relationship had now become very strained to the point of no return.

Terrell began to see D'Angelo do things and see other people, which made him very jealous because he still had feelings for D'Angelo. This is why I stated earlier to Terrell that he was not to engage in a relationship with D'Angelo. People often times want to blame me for their situations in life when I am not always the one to point the finger toward. I give instructions and guidance. It is literally up to you as the person to make a conscious decision to obey me because I know better. Either way, I will still be there to help you through it because that is the type of God that I am.

D'Angelo really did hate Terrell, but loved him at the same time. They had an enlightening conversation in December of 2008 about their feelings for one another and actually had a sexual encounter. Even though this happened, Terrell never told Lavorian about it. Terrell was good at keeping secrets. He rarely kissed and told because he believed in his privacy, but he also did not want to jeopardize what he had, so he thought. There was another man that Terrell had been acquainted with by the name of Miguel. Terrell was in love with Miguel more than he wanted Lavorian. Despite how they felt about one another, he was not aware of the person that Miguel was behind the scenes. Even though Miguel was an older, established man, he was also known to be promiscuous and did not want to pursue a relationship because he was aware of his flaws that he never admitted to. Terrell found out about Miguel through a third party and began to see exactly what the people were saying that informed him about Miguel's behavior. Their relationship never went any further than being close friends.

One thing about Terrell was that he was easily bored with people when in a relationship. If he could not be entertained, he always found that other characteristic in someone else. That was another reason he had a hard time staying committed to those he was in a relationship with.

During the course of the fall semester of his sophomore year, he realized through prayer and spending time with me that I would not allow him to move back to NJ to teach music at his former high school as he had planned. I had a greater plan for him and that was to learn how to work better and relate to people. Therefore, I had him change his major in December 2008 to Sociology. Sociology and music are on two different ends of the spectrum; however, this would be the area that I would use him for a greater purpose.

Even though Terrell was concerned about graduating on time, I already had the master plan. The only thing that I needed him to do was be obedient, which he was. In January 2009, he officially made his switch to Sociology. He removed himself from the concert choir and began to acclimate himself to his new field. He was really in love with his new department and the classes that he was taking. He learned during this first semester in his new major what it meant to be a Sociologist and a Psychologist. He enjoyed his semester and how his life was transforming for the better.

Terrell was in class with this young man named Donovan who was more of Terrell's type. He had brown skin and was very smart which is not to degrade Lavorian however, it was something that caught Terrell's attention. From their interactions with one another, they became friends who ended up having sex with one another. Again, Terrell did not say anything about what had happened, but Donovan did share with some others that they had great sex, which ended up falling on Lavorian's ears.

"Terrell, I just got some disturbing news," said Lavorian. "I heard that you have been having sex with Donovan. Is this true?"

At this point, Terrell was shaken and feared for Lavorian leaving him.

"Hell, no I didn't sleep with him," replied Terrell angrily because he knew he had been caught. "Where did you hear that? Let me call you back after I call him to see what in the world is going on."

He then proceeded to call Donovan,

"Hey man," he said. "Did you tell people that we were having sex?"

"Umm, yeah I did," replied Donovan. "I do not see what the big deal is. You were not saying anything when you were beating it up, so I don't understand what the problem is now."

"Well, my boyfriend found out and I did not tell him that we had been talking," replied Terrell.

"Well I didn't know that you had a boyfriend so that is not my problem," replied Donovan.

"You are right, man, but we can't do this anymore," said Terrell "I hope this doesn't hurt your feelings." After that conversation, Terrell did not know what to do. He had been caught in his own mess without a toilet to flush it down. There are only so many secrets that a person can keep before they come out. Terrell then proceeded to send a long text message to Lavorian, which I was very pleased with because he actually came clean about what he did. Later that evening, there was an event taking place in the auditorium on campus. Terrell saw Lavorian walk in the auditorium and turned his head.

Lavorian decided to sit next to Terrell and told him, "I forgive you, Terrell. I do love you and still want to be with you".

This made Terrell feel good because he really felt as though there was someone that loved him unconditionally through his flaws and all. This was a nice gesture for Lavorian, but the truth is that Terrell did not know the full truth about what Lavorian had been doing, which we will revisit soon.

During that same spring semester, Terrell decided to go out for a fraternity called Phi Iota Omicron. This fraternity had caught Terrell's attention by what they displayed as men, but also because they were heavily looking at him. During the spring of his first year, he went to one of their parties extremely drunk and had to be carried out because he passed out and vomited everywhere. His church friends were very disgusted with him, but others that did not know him showed more compassion than his own friends did. Yes, it is good to have people in your life to hold you accountable for whatever it is that you profess to be, but at the same time, no one has the right to turn their nose up at another person. Love on them and figure out what is wrong so they can get the help that they need. Everyone is human and is subject to error unless they are I, which no one else is.

Anyway, during the time that Terrell went out for the fraternity, he had no idea what he was getting into during spring of 2009. There were about 50 guys from around campus that came to the interest meeting. However, out of that number only six were chosen, with Terrell being one in the number. After the intense process of interviewing, he and the other five were called into their first meeting. Even though Terrell knew that hazing happened with organizations, he always swore to me that he would never go through any of that.

With the conversations of those persons already a part of the fraternity, Terrell and his line brothers were told that they all had to endure the pledge process even though it was illegal. They all came to a consensus and did what was necessary for the process. In three days, the line went from six to four. One boy dropped the first night and the other one did not have the money to pay the organization to continue with the process. Terrell did not have the money either at the time, but one of his roommates had the money stashed because he was not chosen. He gave the money to Terrell in a loan to continue the process. Terrell really did appreciate Mark because he was a genuine person.

During the course of being on line, many things happened to Terrell. Most of all, he began to change into someone that I had not ordained him to be. When a person is in physical pain, it affects their entire person in a negative way. The people that were inflicting the damage would do this while they were drunk and high. These spirits began to transfer into Terrell and there were many days walking on campus that he did not know whether he was going or coming. Because Terrell was an icon on campus, people noticed that he looked different and was acting different. Administration became concerned and so did his friends. Even though some knew what was going on, he was not trying to jeopardize what he had worked hard for at this point.

The one person that dropped line the first night was going around campus telling people about the hazing. This caused the fraternity to be put under investigation. The four that were left including Terrell were called into an interrogation at random times. Terrell lied for the fraternity because he did not want to go to jail or see anyone go to jail. Even with all of the lies, the fraternity was called to go on cease and desist which means there was to be no more activity until further notice. Then there was a judgment made that caused the chapter to be suspended exactly one week before intake.

Terrell did all that he could by writing letters and begging that the chapter not be suspended because there was no hazing that was going on. The members of the fraternity knew that Terrell was working hard because he really wanted to be a part of the organization. Even with all of his efforts, he was not able to cross into the fraternity at that time. Now, of course, he was mad at me because he did not understand why I would allow him to go through all of that and not be able to receive the blessing of it. I told Terrell that he made me a promise and I was not going to allow him to make a mockery of me. He did not understand it at first, but once the chapter was suspended, he began to see the true colors of those who would have been his prophytes. They turned on Terrell fast and did not speak to him. They actually were the ones who were lying on him to the university and stating that he was the one who had told about the hazing when they knew he had not. The thing about Terrell that the fraternity members did not like was that he was always his own person. He told them during one of their nightly sessions, "I don't need this fraternity. I am already an individual and people know me by name, not just by what I am affiliated with". This enraged some of the members because most of them just crossed to gain an identity, but I had already given Terrell an identity that no organization could suppress.

There was still much that Terrell had to learn about himself and it was not the proper time to be a part of this organization. The stages that I set are major and this was not a major stage. During the course of this spring semester, Terrell's GPA dropped to a 2.5, which was the lowest it had been since attending college. He had to work on pulling his grades up in the coming semester and Lavorian was right by his side through all of this turmoil. He was grateful that he and Lavorian were together even though they had their issues, but they did everything together. They really became close friends throughout their relationship and Terrell thought that everything would work out fine between the two of them, however, it did not.

In the summer of 2009, I told Terrell that he must move to South Carolina. He was obedient to what I told him to do, which I was pleased with. He went home to NJ to visit and packed his stuff without knowing where he would be going. He signed up for summer school at CU, but did not have a place to live. He was staying with a friend an hour away from school with no job at the time. The commute became too much for him so he went to the city that his school was in. He and Lavorian were attending summer school together, however, staying on the college campus cost more than living off campus.

Terrell had all of his clothes in his car. At the end of the day, he would sneak into the dorm hall and sleep in an empty dorm room because he had no place to stay. He made this known to some at his church, but no one was willing to lend a helping hand, which was not the Christian thing to do. However, I took care of Terrell. He was working in the admissions office, going to class and his grades were exceptional. During that time, he was also working at a retail store. When he started working at the store, he told the manager of the store, "I was sent here for your life to be saved". The store manager was a woman named Ingrid and she looked at him in disbelief and carried on with her duties.

As time progressed, Ingrid began to listen to Terrell as he would minister to her and she knew that something about this young boy was different. When things became too extreme with the dormitory and not having anywhere to stay, Ingrid opened up her home to Terrell. Ingrid at this time was a mother of two girls and Terrell slept on the couch. While there with her, he continued to do as I said and she ended up coming to church with him one day. As I had informed Terrell to minister to her, I was working on her heart and she came to the ministry. She was filled with me as never before, which I was pleased with and from that point on. I allowed Terrell to move into his own apartment with one of his best friends named Damone. You will never see or be grateful for the blessings that I give you unless you have had to work for them. Terrell's obedience to me caused me to move on his behalf. Terrell was still in summer school and learning what it was like to take responsibility. Now that he had his own place, it was such a relief not living on campus and to have privacy. Being that Lavorian was with Terrell, he did come and stay with Terrell the majority of the time, but there were two situations that began to break the relationship between Terrell and Lavorian.

One situation that occurred during that summer was a woman who was Lavorian's music teacher in high school named Shontell. This woman was a former student at CU, but she was in her 30's. Terrell could not understand why she would be around college students. She was older, but very immature.

One night, Shontell made it known that she was in love with Lavorian and that they had been having sex. Terrell could not believe this to be true because he knew that Lavorian just would not do that. Terrell did not say anything at that time, but he did when Shontell called his phone to confront him about his relationship with Lavorian. She was so hurt because the man that she loved, that was not her husband, was with another man. Apparently, in the past, she had always attracted gay men, so this was a hard experience for her. She had her husband get involved and threaten Terrell, but he was not scared. After he cursed Shontell and her husband out, he went forth to file a police report on her, banning her from the university. She was really a stalker. This situation caused a severance in Lavorian and Terrell's relationship.

In addition, Terrell had gotten back into the mode of checking Lavorian's social media accounts and his cell phone as he had done with Rommelle. During his search, he discovered that Lavorian was having a relationship with Miguel. Lavorian was coming across strong to Miguel and he knew that they were friends. In Terrell's rage before he went to work his other job as a waiter, he confronted Lavorian who denied everything.

Upon Terrell's return from work, Lavorian was gone. He left a letter on the bed stating that he was leaving due to Terrell's controlling behavior, but Terrell knew that was not the only reason. Now that Lavorian had used him, he was of no more use. This really did hurt Terrell along with everything else that was going on in his personal life. He never would have thought that Lavorian would leave him, but everyone else around Terrell knew that he was being used. When a person is in love, it will cause them to do some crazy things for the one they love. People believe that I am crazy too because I came from glory to human flesh, just to die so that you are who are reading this book could live. How crazy, right?

During the time that the fall of 2009 came around, Terrell began to experience what it really meant to be an adult. He was living in an apartment where bills had to be paid and food had to be cooked. There were times where he and his roommate did not have the money to pay rent nor pay utility bills, which caused him to seek public assistance. There were many times that Terrell and his roommate had received eviction notices from their racist property owner. This caused Terrell to seek help from places such as the Salvation Army and other entities where he would have to be outside at two in the morning just to try to make sure that he would be able to get assistance when the company opened at 8am. By the time Terrell got to the door some days, he was told that the company was not serving any more people. This was very heart wrenching for him as he was trying to figure out how he could live without making the necessary money.

Along with the issues that he was dealing with, Terrell had befriended another person named Antwon. Antwon was older than Terrell but they both connected on multiple levels. Antwon was very courageous and he learned how to handle Terrell with all of his character flaws. During the course of their friendship, there were deeper feelings that had been established. In the midst of the feelings that were known for one another, Terrell was still not over Lavorian.

During the course of his junior year of college from fall 2009 to spring 2010, Terrell was on a seesaw with Lavorian. Lavorian left CU to go and allegedly stay with his godmother, but Terrell found out through my intervention that Lavorian was lying to him. Another guy had graduated from CU who Lavorian was friends with and did not tell Terrell. Terrell would drive from SC to Raleigh, NC whenever Lavorian needed him. From NC, he followed Lavorian to Atlanta where he hoped their relationship would rekindle. All the time that he was going back and forth with Lavorian, Terrell was still in a friendship with Antwon, who was patiently waiting on him.

Antwon and Terrell had many great times together. Most of the time, Terrell felt as though when he was in relationships, he was the teacher. I connected him with Antwon because it was necessary for his growth and development. Antwon was also a member of the fraternity that Terrell wanted to be a part of. In spring 2010, Terrell went back out for the fraternity and this time he was denied membership. He tried to argue with the men of the fraternity because he knew that their judging process was flawed, however, there was no avail for Terrell. The reason being was that they knew at this point that Terrell would not be willing to sell his soul just to be a member of an organization. They were looking for people who would sell themselves in order to put on this new identity.

Terrell watched 15 men cross into the fraternity that he had wanted to be a part of. One of the things that really bothered Terrell was that all of the ones that were chosen with the exception of one had been denied the year before. This helped Terrell understand that this particular chapter of the fraternity was not looking for quality but they were looking for quantity. They were looking for someone who would be willing to sacrifice their wellbeing just to have some letters across their chest. Terrell was always an individual and I told him that he did not need letters to validate who he was as a man. Many men do not really accept the fact that there is an important factor to male affirmation. When their fathers or another male figure that stands proxy in the absence of their dad does not affirm them, men look for affirmation in other areas. This can be very troubling, but this is an issue that men need to learn to address.

I will take this moment and tell every man who is reading this that I love you for who you are because I created you. Stop looking for the affirmation and validation of other people because there is a strong chance that you will never find it. My approval and validation is really all that matters.

When you pass along this journey called life, there will come a day where you will have to meet me face-to-face. During this encounter, I am not going to ask, "Why didn't your parent/guardian approve you?" I will ask you what you did with the time that I have given you to be the best individual that I have called you to be. Nevertheless, I digress and retract to Terrell.

Terrell really desired to be affirmed because it was something that he was lacking. Even in his times of tragedy and accomplishments, there was still much work for him to do. During the spring of his junior year, Terrell was having a conversation with Ingrid.

"Hey, how are you doing today?" he asked her.

"I am doing all right," replied Ingrid. "Just had a busy day at work."

"Well, how are the girls and how is Taylor doing?" asked Terrell.

At this time, Ingrid only had two children, but I was speaking through Terrell to get a message to Ingrid. While Terrell was in his kitchen cooking, I gave him these words to speak to Ingrid.

"Ingrid, I know that you already have girls, but the Lord said that you are going to have a son and you have to call him Taylor. Taylor is going to be the one to save your life and the anointing on his life will be so great that it will influence the lives of many. Don't worry about your current situation because your child will not want for anything."

When Terrell shared my word with Ingrid, she did not believe him at all because she was not trying to have any additional children. However, the next month, Ingrid called Terrell to tell him that she was pregnant. She was crying and wanted to abort the baby because she did not believe that she could provide an efficient life for the child. I used Terrell to minister to her spirit and coach her along the process.

During the time of her pregnancy, the biological father of the child left her once he found out she was pregnant. He did not want to have anything to do with the child. Regardless, he was just used to produce the seed. I had already told Ingrid that the child would not want for anything and that is what I meant.

While having these prophetic encounters with me, I sent Terrell to NJ on assignment to minister to his mother. During that time, he was working at a restaurant, but had to go home before summer school for 2010. When I sent him home, it was because I showed him his mother as being like Lot's wife. If she did not stop turning back to the past, she would perish. This was a very hard thing to do because Terrell and his mother did not have an in-depth conversation about her life nor the struggles that she faced.

As Terrell was home in NJ with his parents on a thirteen day assignment, I put him to work. I gave him words to speak every day to his parents and work through sessions with them so that his mother could be delivered. When people are in trouble, I will always send help. Terrell felt as though he was inadequate because he was the child, but I used him as the child to see his mother reborn. At the end of the hard assignment, Terrell's mother began to acknowledge him as the anointed man that he had always been. It took me sending him to N.J. for his mother and family not to view him anymore as just their son, but also as the prophet to bring order, correction, instruction, and deliverance.

Terrell was astonished because in all of his years of living, his mother never publicly acknowledged the anointing on him until he had to come and minister to her. This was such a breaking point in his mother's life and it was necessary for what was to come in the near future.

As time continued to progress, I was with Terrell. He was a minister in training at his church in SC and served in many different areas, but that was not all. Even in his holy state, he still did not know how to properly let go of people and things that served him no purpose. One thing that Terrell learned as a behavior was how to hold on to what you have even when it is not productive. He still chased after Lavorian. Even though I sent someone else who treated him better than he had been treated in times past, he still wanted to return to a dead relationship.

During the fall of 2010, Terrell had many things going on. He was trying to graduate early from college, while working hard and figuring out different things in life. While preparing to graduate, he did not know what his next move was until he was having a conversation with one of his professors.

"Terrell, you are called to be a pastor and you need to go to seminary," his professor told him. "Every time we talk about religion or something pertaining to God in our Sociology classes, you just light up. You need to do what you have been called to do instead of wrecking your brain and wasting time doing what you want. God does not always operate on what you want, but more of what he wants from you."

This spoke to Terrell's spirit because he knew that this was the truth. Terrell had been applying to schools, but he was not sure as to where he was going to go.

He was accepted to a theological school in Atlanta, which is where he was planning on going in December 2010. After he was done with classes, he did go to Atlanta to stay for a week. While he was there, he tried to figure out if there was any chance for him and Lavorian to rekindle their relationship. After spending a week there, and Lavorian using Terrell, their relationship actually ended. Lavorian treated Terrell in a terrible manner while he was there and just used him for money and sex. Terrell made up in his mind that once he left this time, he was not returning to this situation. He made this clear to Lavorian, who was not concerned with Terrell at all (or so he said to others). Terrell packed his bag and proceeded to leave Lavorian's apartment.

As he began to walk down the hallway, he began to sing, "I am free. Praise the Lord, I'm free. No longer bound, no more chains holding me. My soul is resting, it's just a blessing. Praise the Lord, Hallelujah I'm free."

At this point, Terrell had made a decision to be free, and now I was able to do some much needed work. People often say that they want to be delivered, but I cannot deliver them until they want it bad enough. There has to come a time when you as people relinquish your will so that my will can be done in your life. My ways are always better, by the way.

While he was leaving Atlanta, I spoke to him and informed him that it would not be smart to leave SC now. Not only because I had additional work for him to do, but also because he was trying to move for a negative reason. As Terrell was back in SC, without knowing what was going to happen to him pertaining to employment and life, I had him go on a consecration. Some things will only be broken by fasting and praying to me. Therefore, Terrell prayed to me and sought me because he had a soul tie to Lavorian that needed to be broken.

It is amazing that people cannot move forward in life because of who their souls are connected to. In order to be free and to move on, one must release their soul tie to the person or people that they have connected to. Terrell had a desire even in all of this to please me. He knew that his relationship with Lavorian was toxic and that it needed to end. He was becoming a person that I had not intended for him to become. This is why I was proud of Terrell be cause he began to live his truth. He understood that it was nobody but me who had brought him this far and I would be the only one to take him further.

Terrell made it through his undergraduate years because of me. Through his trials, tribulations and good times, he was able to finish CU early. He had grown so much and had accomplished so many things. I was proud of him. Even though I knew that I was proud of him, he did not think the same because of his flaws. Flaws will always cause people to miss me in the fullness of my deity. Because of what people know about themselves, they believe that they should be perfect when that is not realistic. Man was perfect during the initial construction through Adam, but the nature of man has fallen since the Garden of Eden. This is why I came down to become flesh, so that people like you who find yourself in these situations can understand that I am the truth, the way, and the life. I am just waiting on you to accept me as I have already accepted and loved you.

CHAPTER 10
The Truth

Happy New Year! It is January 2011 and I have such interesting plans for Terrell. He graduated early from CU and was now a mature young adult, living on his own. He was applying for many jobs, but did not seem to receive any calls. On January 12, 2011, Ingrid gave birth to the promise that he had prophesied about.

TJ was born as a healthy big baby boy, and Terrell was delighted. He went to the hospital the next day to see the manifestation. Could you imagine seeing a living being that I told you to speak into existence and it actually shows up? This was so fulfilling for Terrell, because this baby gave him the life that he needed in order to trust me even more. Ingrid was pleased to have a son as well.

Over the course of the next few months, Terrell and Antwon were still dating and living life without any cares. Terrell did get a job as a retail manager and several months later, transitioned to working in education as his heart desired. In February of that year, Terrell received a very interesting Facebook message from Lavorian that read:

"Hey Terrell. I hope that you are doing well. I just want to let you know that I am so sorry for the way that I treated you and for lying to you as much as I have. I realized over these past two months that I made a huge mistake. I have been living in Atlanta for a while and realized that there is no one that will love me as you did. I hope that you can find it in your heart to forgive me and maybe we can work on making things better."

As Terrell was reading this message, he could not do anything but laugh. This was hilarious to him, as it was to me as well. Terrell knew that even with all of his issues, he was genuinely a good person, and good people are hard to find. Terrell responded back by saying:

"Thank you for your message. However, our relationship is over. When I walked out of your apartment after you told me that you did not want anything else to do with me, I was done. I prayed and asked God to break the soul tie that I had to you and he did just that. I would be a fool to return to my own vomit. You do not deserve me or another chance. We can be cordial to one another, but you are no longer a priority in my life. God Bless you."

What I loved about his statement was that he was being honest about where he was in life. He was not seeking after Lavorian because Antwon was taking great care of him at this point. Terrell was living alone, what he thought to be a great life.

As time progressed, Terrell relocated to another city in SC where he began to thrive and get very involved. He was prospering and was waiting for graduation from CU. Even though he did finish a semester early, CU only had one graduation, which was in May of each year. During the months of April and May, Terrell was able to attend many different activities with his senior class and accepted for summer intake to the fraternity that he was on line for during his undergraduate career. He was so excited about life, but he realized that he had not been living truthfully.

As much as Terrell loved his mother, he never officially told her about his truth because he did not want to disappoint her. Many of you reading this have not been living your truth. Instead, the choice has been made to live a lie because of the same reason that Terrell did--"Fear of Rejection". This is another reason why having a relationship with me is so important because I too was rejected. Even in my rejection by those who I thought loved me, so many others were granted eternal life and the chance to know me personally.

After graduation from CU in May 2011, Terrell and his mother went for a walk by the river and he decided to tell her the truth. It was not shocking to her, but she was hurt.

Even in her hurt, she told him these very important words. "Son, I still love you. What happens in your life is between you and God. I did the best that I could to raise you, but I understand that others do not always accept the people that we love. As long as you are happy, I am happy. You are my son and I value you for who you are because you help me to see life from a different perspective."

Terrell was happy to have this conversation with his mother and that she now knew that he was dating Antwon. Life was seemingly getting better for him until he received a phone call from his estranged brother in North Carolina.

In the month of June 2011, Terrell had one of the most difficult conversations with his brother about his sexuality. The terrible part was that his brother was 30+, with no education beyond high school and was barely able to take care of himself. He was also a minister. Let us keep in mind that his brother did not reach out to him during the course of the years, but always remained in his own secluded world. It was not until Terrell's father told him about his sexual orientation that he reached out.

When Terrell's mom and dad were en route back to NJ, his mother told his dad about Terrell. She then blamed his father for not being there and said that he was the reason that Terrell was the way that he was because he was not an active part of Terrell's life. Contrary to popular belief, it is not because of the absence of a father that a person identifies as something different sexually. It can be a factor, but not the main factor. Nevertheless, Terrell and his brother got into an intense argument. One of the things that Terrell's brother said to him was, "You can't call yourself a preacher or be helping anyone and you a fucking faggot. God don't honor that and it is not right. Daddy is down here telling me about this stuff and he is really upset with you."

Take a moment to put yourself in Terrell's shoes. Your family member calls you and bashes you about your entire life when they do not even know your daily struggles and what it takes just for you to keep your sanity. Words really do affect people. Outside of Terrell's orientation, he was the ideal young man. Very handsome, courageous, educated, saved, anointed, and compassionate just to name a few of his characteristics. Terrell was having an intense verbal exchange with his own blood brother about his sexuality, and he did not use profanity. I was proud of him and I allowed this to be a teachable moment for him because as long as people are imperfect, which will be forever, others will always find error with what you are doing. In doing so, they never take the time to address their own issues. Terrell's brother had and still does have many unresolved issues.

After the conversation with his brother, as Terrell was standing at his kitchen sink preparing dinner, he broke down crying. Antwon was there during the time and he came in to console Terrell, which is exactly what he needed at that time. He was already under a lot of pressure at work, learning the information in preparation for his national exam in a few weeks for the fraternity amongst many other things. I took time to comfort Terrell because this was just the beginning of what he would have to face. It is one thing to be ostracized and ridiculed from the outside world. However, when your own family is doing the damage, it makes it hard to trust anyone.

The next day, Terrell confronted his father. He still honored his father as my word instructs children to do, but he was very vocal about how disappointed he was in his father. He had absolutely no right to go to this brother and not come to him directly. Not only did Terrell's dad go to his other son to spread Terrell's business, but he also told many additional individuals who were a part of his side of the family that Terrell had not had the opportunity to meet. This really hurt Terrell because his own father wanted to run and tell things about him, but would never tell his family how lousy of a husband he was to Terrell's mother. Before this information came to the surface, Terrell's dad always bragged about him to everyone because he had done so much. During their conversation, Terrell mentioned all of this to his dad, yet his dad was not receptive.

"God, you know what? I have done what I can. I can't please everyone and I am not going to try. I am a college graduate, living on my own, paying my own bills and doing the best that I can. You know my heart and you know my life. God, I just need you to help me get through this. I know that better days are ahead and I know that I will make it through this rough time. If my father and brother don't want to claim me because of my sexuality, then so be it. I have gotten to where I am today not because of them, but because of you as well as my other family members. You have given me the ability to live and I choose to live in my truth instead of hiding it. No, everyone does not have to know my business, but I should be able to be honest with my parents."

That was Terrell's prayer to me during this trial and it was the very sentiments of his heart that caused me to move on his behalf.

During the month of July, he went to the national meeting for the fraternity for membership intake. He was scared, but he was determined to be a part of this organization. He went through the various ritualistic programs and crossed the burning sands of the fraternity. Some of those that were attending CU were at the national meeting and did not expect to see him there. I had prepared a huge table before Terrell in the presence of his enemies, and they had no other choice but to dine at his party. Many were jealous and upset, but when I open doors for a person, no one can shut them but me. This was going to be a great year for Terrell and he deserved it.

Once he came back from the national meeting, he was still working and the conditions became very hostile. The management was racist and Terrell began to have many health challenges. With my leading, I told him to resign on 9/1/2011, which is what he did. He felt so relieved and he took some time off to go back to NJ to be with his family.

While in NJ, he sat with his grandmother for a long time. Upon him hugging her, he discerned her spirit was tired. He then began to pray for his grandmother. He loved her dearly. When he returned to SC, he was still actively job searching and attending church in Orangeburg. In October, Terrell got a phone call. Upon returning from dialysis, his grandmother went into cardiac arrest and they revived her five times from Thursday until that Saturday. From there, his grandmother went into a coma and two weeks later, she passed away in the hospital.

The reason why his grandmother did not leave sooner is that she was fighting to remain on the earth. During the time that she was in a coma, Terrell was able to speak to her spirit. I have blessed him with many gifts; one being to speak to a person's spirit even in their unconscious state. He was over 700 miles away, yet because he had a strong connection with me, he could communicate in the spirit realm. His grandmother was sharing with him that she wanted to stay alive because of her sons. They would not be able to make it without her and she was used to being there for everyone else.

Terrell had to help her understand that her sons would be fine and that if she was tired, she should just come home to me.

After much deliberation and fighting to remain on earth, his grandmother gave up her spirit to me. I had shown Terrell back in January that his grandmother would pass away. He did not want to believe it, which is what most people do when I show them things, but I do this so that when it does happen, it does not hurt as much.

During the time that she was transitioning from Earth to glory, I allowed Terrell to see this happening in a dream. She was dressed in pure white with a large smile on her face as she was ascending into the bright light in the sky. As he could only see the light in the dream, his cell phone rang. He was informed that his grandmother had passed away. He got on the road to NJ and cried the entire time. He was upset that his grandmother had passed away, but once he arrived in NJ, he understood that there was still an assignment.

Terrell and one of his sisters planned the entire celebration service for their grandmother. His sister praise danced at the service and Terrell led praise and worship and also gave words on behalf of the family that I told him to share. From his obedience of speaking my word at the home-going service without being the eulogist, people gave their lives to Christ. This helped Terrell to capture a glimpse of how impactful his ministry would be.

Once the home-going service was over, Terrell departed to SC and additional problems arose. Because his grandmother had been so close to him, he did not know how to deal with her death. He started having anxiety attacks really badly during the months of November and December until he went to counseling. He was never prescribed any medicine, but he did trust and know that I would be his comforter during this time of bereavement.

By this time also, he had another job working for another university, which he enjoyed at first, before he realized that his supervisor was trying to get him terminated because she was afraid of Terrell's ability to do her job. When a person does not rightfully belong in a position, they will always be intimidated when they see people who have the skills that they are missing.

Terrell, however, did not allow this to move him because I created him to be much stronger than that. He received a long text message from his brother on Christmas day apologizing for his actions during the summer and he admitted to the fact that he was jealous of Terrell and all of his accomplishments. He could not understand that if Terrell were living this lifestyle, how and why I would be using him the way that I was. As I stated before, I will take the foolish things to confound those who believe they are so wise. It was not meant for him to understand. I know what I am doing.

As Terrell continued throughout his journey going into 2012 and 2013, there were so many additional things for him to encounter. One of those awakening moments was when he finally left the church that he had been a part of for the years that he was in SC. Terrell learned about himself while serving there and also understood that the love that is shown in the church should not just be based on a condition. Though Terrell was very influential, he had more gifts than singing praise and worship. This is a note to all of you who are sitting in churches and not growing. I have not called you to sit and do nothing with your life. The gifts that I have given you should be used for the building of my kingdom. Those who serve as pastors and other authoritative figures in the church are subject to error because they are human just like you.

One thing that is taking place in most churches today is Charismatic Witchcraft. It bothers me that so many of my children are willing to take heed to their Pastor's voice that they cannot even recognize mine. Some are using it for their own personal gain by ensuring that you are broke while they are living lavishly. If you are in a ministry where you are not growing and changing for the better, I beseech you to leave. I would never plant you in a place for you to die when the church is designed to be your place of refuge and change. Understand that your pastor is not me! I am the only one, true and living God and perfect being. Even though the Pastor's are supposed to be the mouthpiece, one must be able to differentiate between my voice and their voices. Pastors, you should also be aware that the people that join your congregations are still my people. I have the power to move my people wherever I want them to go. If they leave and never return, you should still love them as I love you. Even if they do not return, there should not be any malice or false humility when you see them. Put aside your pride and arrogance to show the genuine love of who I am. This is the key to winning souls for my kingdom and not your own.

Once Terrell learned and accepted that it was time to move on, he did just that. Once he was free, he was able to accomplish so much more with his life. He went on to graduate with a Masters degree and he will pursue a doctoral degree in the future. One thing that people must understand is that success, greatness, and the anointing comes with a price. Many desire fame and fortune. The question is; Are you willing to pay the price to be on the platform? Nothing in life is free. Please remember that.

CHAPTER 11
It Comes With a Price

To be anointed and be effective, you have to pay for it. So many want the anointing, but do not want to pay the price for it. The anointing is likened to olive oil. Green olives do not produce the extra virgin olive oil, but it comes from the black olives. Once the olives have grown, they are pressed so that what is in it can be of use to someone else in its purest form. In order to be effective in the lives others, there has to be a pressing in order for the potency of what is in you to be strong enough to impact and change lives around you.

In 2014, I spoke to Terrell in the beginning of the year and told him the following:

"Terrell, you have endured a lot throughout your life and I am pleased with your progress and maturity. In 2015, I will launch you into the deep. Your career, ministry, and life will exceed beyond what you ever thought. In all that I am going to do for you, I can't show you it all, but you will get all that I have for you as long as you remain committed to me and obedient to the call that I have placed on your life without reservation. With all that I am doing through you and for you, I must say this lastly. You will be launched into the deep, but you first will suffer tragic loss."

That was all that I said to Terrell and he was confused as to why I would share with him all of the positive things and then leave him with the fact that he would suffer tragic loss..

In the beginning of the year 2014, I allowed sickness to fall upon him and he had never been as sick as this. What started as a sinus infection turned into a more severe sickness, which caused him to be out of commission for almost two months. During this time, he could do nothing but seek me, which is what he did. He became even more grateful for the activities of his limbs because there was a time during his sickness where he could barely walk. After being healed from having a severe strand of the flu, he continued working his secular job and doing ministry. He started working on a doctoral program and was so excited about it. During this entire time, he was conversing heavily with his family about the things that he was doing and then Terrell got some very troubling news. While pursuing his doctorate degree during the summer of 2014, he got a call from NJ that his mother had gotten sick and was in the hospital. This alarmed Terrell because his mother was hospitalized once before due to her ankle being broken.

Terrell, being over 700 miles away from home, became concerned, but did not stress about it too much. He figured that his mother would recover as she had in times past. As Terrell was enjoying his doctoral program, he was able to speak with his mother even though she could not talk much. She was having some lung problems and it prohibited her from speaking as much as she normally would. She could barely state a sentence without coughing and becoming winded. She was released from the hospital and Terrell was told that she was on oxygen, which concerned him, but again, having faith in me, he did not want to think of the worse scenarios.

In August, he went to go and visit his Godparents that stayed in Georgia for a weekend. He had not seen them in a few years and wanted to check on them because I dropped it in his spirit that he needed to go and spend some time with them. As Terrell was in Georgia visiting, he enjoyed his God-family and I used him during that time to speak life into the lives of the saints of a church that he visited. Upon his return back to SC, he received a phone call on August 18 from the hospital in NJ.

The lung specialist told him, "Terrell, you need to come up here and see your mother because she is not in good condition."

Terrell and the doctor had an exchange because Terrell did not know that his mother was as ill as she was. Even in speaking with his sisters, no one seemed to have known what was going on.

The next day in the early morning, Terrell drove from SC to NJ to see about his mother. As he was thirty miles away from the hospital, he got a call from the hospital that informed him that his mother was transferred to the intensive care unit because she could not breathe. Terrell then began to drive quickly to reach the hospital because he was not sure what was going on. Once he arrived at the hospital, he rushed to see his mother and when he did, he was not prepared for what he would see.

When he entered the room where his mother was on that Tuesday, she was awake, but unable to speak. She had a breathing mask on her face and she looked bad. Terrell was keeping his composure because he did not want to show his weakness in front of his mother. His mother was terrified because she did not know what was going on and so was Terrell.

During that time, he prayed for his mother and stayed there for the rest of the day until that evening. While he was there, he had meetings with a number of physicians who then told him that his mother was very ill. What started as a sinus infection for her, turned into double bacterial pneumonia and acute respiratory distress syndrome. To make those terms plain, her lungs had failed. She could not breathe on her own, which was why she was on oxygen. This news devastated Terrell. He then became the point of contact for his mother. He had to sign papers of consent being that his mother was unable to and during that time, he felt as though he was signing her life away.

The first night in NJ, he did not want to sleep in his mother's apartment because he knew that it would be too emotional so he stayed with one of his friends that night.

Over the next few days, Terrell's mother got worse. On that Wednesday, she had to get a lung biopsy and as he watched her roll away into the operating room, Terrell broke down sobbing. The emotions were so intense because he and his mother were like best friends. A nurse pulled him aside and she prayed for him. While his mother was in the operating room, Terrell was in the chapel of the hospital praying for his mother. When she came out of surgery, she was in distress, which traumatized Terrell. He could see that his mother was in so much pain. They had to put her back to sleep to ensure that she did not try to remove the tubes that they had going down her throat. Over the next two days, her condition got worse. They had to transport her from one hospital to another and Terrell was not happy about that. The room that they transferred her to was in the same hospital that his grandmother had passed away in and on the exact same floor.

The doctors had to transfer her because they specialized in lung care. From that Tuesday through that Saturday, Terrell saw his mother go from being alert, to lying on a bed lifeless. She was on life support, E.C.M.O, and many other machines just to keep her stable. During this time, Terrell was cleaning her apartment little by little because he was not sure how this situation would turn out. Her apartment was cold and lifeless as well because she had not been there since about early July.

Terrell stayed for one week then traveled back to SC. While he was there, he cried every day. I reminded him of the tragic loss conversation that took place earlier in the year. He still believed for his mother's healing on this side because he did not know how he would continue to live without her. Everything that he did in life was to make his mother happy. He was making a living so that she could move down south with him and he could take care of her since his father did not do a good job of being her husband. His dad left NJ and his wife after Terrell's grandmother passed away in 2011. This caused Terrell to harbor resentment against his father because he was just not a good example, neither did he take care of his mother the way Terrell knew she should have been taken care of.

Terrell left NJ because he agreed at that time with whatever my will would be for his mother's life. As time progressed, he kept the faith and went back to work. He was excited about teaching at the college and serving his community, until he got some additional news. His mother was awake, but could not talk because of the tubes that were in her body. He was able to speak to her over the phone and tried to remain positive by telling her that her sickness was not unto death. She would write messages down and his sister would relay those to him. Terrell's birthday was on 9/12 and he was planning to have a grand celebration of life. Instead, he spent his birthday in the funeral home in Newark, NJ planning the funeral for his mother who passed away on Wednesday 9/10. His mother went into septic shock in less than 24 hours causing her organs to fail.

When Terrell got the call from his sister Gabriel, who had been in the hospital for their mother and grandmother's last breath, he lost it. That Wednesday, he was at work and the grief that hit him was unexplainable. He was at work when he got the news and he was on the ground screaming. He traveled to NJ the next morning and immediately went to the hospital to pull his mother's body from the morgue. She looked like she was resting, but Terrell could not believe that his mother was gone. He tapped her body to feel that it was ice cold and there was no life left in her body. On the day that his mother passed, he told me these words:

"God, you let my mother pass two days before my birthday. How could you do this to me? For all of these years, I have been living and trying to do what is right, and you take away the one person that I know loved me unconditionally. Why would you do this to me? You know what, I am not preaching anymore. I am not doing anything pertaining to you because this is not fair. You should not have done this to me. Who am I going to talk to now? Who is going to show me love like my mother? No one. She is gone and you took her. I know that you said that I would suffer a tragic loss, but I did not want it to be my mother. How could you do this to me? Are you not considerate of my feelings and my life? I can't live without my mother. I won't curse you because I know that I shouldn't, but just know that I do not agree with your will at this time."

Terrell had every right to be angry. He wanted to enjoy his birthday and hear his mother's voice and not be planning a funeral for her. What he did not know was that all of this had such a purpose for his life. At the funeral home, the family discovered that there was no life insurance and this hurt Terrell as well as his sisters. Terrell was just ready to get this over with, but I had a plan during the process..

Once the family left the funeral home, Terrell continued to stay in his mother's apartment and he had to clean through decades of stuff that his mother had. Can you imagine his emotional state? He was grieving while being angry with me and everyone else. His dad came up from Florida and Terrell did not like that at first because he figured that if his dad had been a good husband, his mother would not have passed away.

Terrell had many emotions to work through and life was indeed very trying for him. When a person passes away, there is still business that has to be handled. While Terrell was handling the business aspect, he was tasked by me to preach his mother's eulogy. At first, he told me no, but I reminded him that even in death, he still has to be obedient to my will. He agreed to do what

I told him to do and he informed the Pastor of their home church that he was going to preach the funeral. His current Pastor gave him his blessing and things were moving forward. The days leading to his mother's celebration of life was very trying, as he and his dad were not getting along. I had to work on Terrell during this time because he was starting to develop hate towards his dad again. In reality, he began to blame his dad for his mother's death. I had to remind Terrell that this battle was not for him to fight, but he had to forgive his father and still show him my love.

On September 19th, the body of Terrell's mother was laid to rest. The service was wonderful and this was everyone's first time hearing Terrell preach since his first message when he accepted the call in 2006. I really did use him on that day. As hard as it was for him, I gave him strength to endure. When people are weak, that gives me the opportunity to be strong on their behalf. My strength is made perfect during times of weakness. This helps the person understand that they cannot do everything on their own and that I am needed for the journey.

Later that evening, after his mother's body was committed to the ground, his father was rushed to the hospital because he had gotten sick. The following morning, some of his cousins were robbed at gunpoint. What a day? He would listen to Gospel artist Jessica Reedy every day with her debut song *Better*. This song helped him to get through the rough times that were happening to him. Even through this, I was still working on his behalf and the family's. Once everything was said and done, Terrell was able to go back to SC and then trouble hit.

Terrell began to have anxiety attacks again. When all of the text messages, phone calls and emails stop, a person still has to deal with the truth of life as it is. Thus, when Terrell got back to SC, he had his first anxiety attack since December 2011, and it was bad. The grief began to get to him even though he was trying to focus on the positive things in life. He was traumatized. The mental images of seeing his mother sick and now deceased were very traumatic and became a reoccurring nightmare. Here is an entry that Terrell wrote:

Mental Image

Every time I close my eyes
Mental images I despise
Seeing you was hard
Not seeing you at all anymore hurts
Crying because I miss every ounce of your being
However, that does not stop me from seeing,
Seeing you afraid of what was to come
Not even knowing this battle, you already won
Plugged up to machines, yet I was the one
It was hard to sign your life away as your only son

Who would have thought you would leave so soon?
Now many of my days are filled with gloom
You were getting better so we thought
But God came and you got caught
Caught up to see him in his majesty
While leaving us on Earth to bare the tragedy
Tragedy of watching your body committed to the ground
I feel lost without you, even though you have been found

I woke up with images of your corpse

Haunting me every day without recourse

My mother, my homie, my friend,

All I have now are mental images to hold me and mend

Mend my brokenness that is unexplainable

I wonder if my future is even attainable

From a hospital bed to a casket

I feel like I am going to blow a gasket

I just want to be where you are

It would make me feel better than being so far

Memories, memories, memories

That is all I have

Prayerfully they can one day make me laugh

I wanted to see you alive and well

But this, dear mom, feels like hell

The excruciating knowledge that you are not here

Causes me to live in fear

You were a huge part of my world

Now transitioned on to another

Mental images, thoughts and emotions

Bring me to a place of acceptance and coping

This is my prayer Lord…and I am hoping that I will eventually stop moping

The mourning process for Terrell was intense. He now had to live without his mother. There were many hard days for him, but he was making it through them. He dealt with many different emotions and much rage. He was also able to see how in all of this, I was making him into the man that I called him to be. The funeral of his mother was prophetic and I reminded him that it had been 9 years since he first preached his first message. He stood in the same pulpit to preach his initial sermon and I wanted to show him that there was still work to do.

As the next few months progressed, he was still having anxiety attacks and thought about doing many deviant things. There came a time where he was drinking every night just to go to sleep until he was reminded that doing this would not bring his mother back. He picked the pen back up and began to write about his life and his feelings. He wrote another poem entitled "Final Words" that reads:

As I reflect over the past few months, I came across words
Words of Despair
Words of Anxiety
Words of Fear
Words of Faith, yet hopeless

I heard you go from positive thoughts to not being sure whether you would live or die
In your confused state, I assured you that you would live.
I gave you hope, but I don't know what for
Our last text was on 8/17 and in a matter of 3 weeks, the last words stand strong
I expressed my love to you, but that doesn't fill the void of not being able to hear from
you
What does a person do when the last words are literally "Last Words"?
A final expression of feelings has to last with a person for the rest of their lives

Words that have power are always attached to one of the most intimate moments of a person's life

I wish and pray that my last words would have been longer

I wish that I didn't have to share those words under those circumstances

So many feelings and unanswered questions go along with the "Last Words"

However, life has to move beyond the last words. Gone, but not forgotten. I love you

As Terrell was coping with the death of his mother, he was not prepared for the additional news that he received in November. One night, as he was in bed, he became overwhelmed with grief. He began listening to Tasha Cobbs and kept playing *For your Glory*. He had no idea why this was happening, but he knew that when he experienced things like this, someone close to him had passed away.

The next day, he got a phone call stating that his Godmother that he had just seen in August had passed away.

"God, are you serious?" he said.

This was a lot for him to handle and he did not hold up his strength during the funeral of his Godmother, who was buried exactly two months after his mother. Terrell continued to grieve, but he realized that he could not stay at the grave too long. He made a decision that he had to turn his grief into celebration even in his despair and hurt. In order for me to launch him the way that I promised him, he had to be pressed, broken, shaken, and torn down in order for me to build him back up.

Through all of these trials and tribulations, I have proven to be with Terrell. Many days, he thought he would not make it, but this is just a testimony that I am a keeper. Everything that I do is for a purpose that is greater than what you can ever imagine. Terrell trusted me and obeyed even when he did not understand. This was all happening so that the greatness that is in him could come forth. Even in death, he received a burst of new life. Not a sad story, but a testament as to why having a personal relationship with me is important. Today, Terrell stands strong and is in such a phenomenal place in life. Through the test and trials of time, Terrell was able to make it and so are you.

CHAPTER 12
You Can Make It

Romans 8:1 reads, *"There is therefore now no condemnation to them which are in Christ Jesus, who walk not after the flesh, but after the Spirit."* The reason why so many people travel through life not having a relationship with me is that they feel condemned. Certain religious people are preaching and teaching that message. If I was not who I am, I would think that obtaining a relationship with me would be unattainable as well. However, that is not the case. I did not come to condemn the world, nor the people that I have placed in it. I came to save.

Terrell had and will continue to have issues just as you who are reading this book will. The question is do you really want to have a relationship with me? I am waiting for you to be honest about who you are because I already know. There is no need to put on a façade because that does not carry any weight. I would much rather you be who I designed you to be instead of putting on this costume so that others can accept you. With all of the different trials that Terrell endured, I was with him. As I was with him, I want you to know that I am with you also. Your struggles are designed for you to get to know me better. Had Terrell not endured these things, he would not know me for who I am authentically. Most people just seek me for what I can do, which is a very fleshly perspective, instead of getting to know me for who I am. I am more than what my hand provides. There is a big difference. Deliverance is possible if you really want it, but know that it happens in my timing. I take the foolish things of life to confuse the wise. Most Christians believe that they have me figured out and know how I am going to move when that is absurd. I am God. I move the way that I want to, when I want to and I will use whom I choose. I wanted Terrell to know that I love him for who he is, along with his struggles. I am the one who has allowed this to happen in his life. Even though people do not understand his life or why I am using him to this capacity, it is not any of their concern. If they would turn off their eyes of flesh and turn on their spiritual eyes, then they would be able to see things more clearly and see more things of me instead of magnifying the flesh to a state it should not be.

I love Terrell with all of my heart and with all of my soul. I love him so because I created him and I am happy that he is not the same person he once was.. He has come so far and he loves me so much, but I love him even more. I am proud of the progress that he is making through the fires of life. He is learning to live life for himself in freedom. Because of this, I am able to use him much more than when he was struggling to remain in societal norms. In my word, I tell everyone that all things are possible through me. Know that your total submission and obedience to what I have called you to do will cause you to commune with me. Sometimes the work that I call people to do is not popular, but it is effective. It is my hope that while reading this text, you were able to see yourself somehow and someway. Not only that, but I also pray on your behalf that you open the eyes of your heart and begin to view yourself and others the way that I view them. In reality, it is only my view of a person that matters. It is fine to live a life that people do not understand. They did not create you, I did. Life is about choices and I pray that you choose to live. Do not just live to be existing, but live life more abundantly in your truth. Adam and Eve tried to live a lie amongst many others in current society and you are able to see what happens to them when they live a false life. While man focuses on your outward, I am more focused on your heart.

What holds many people back from living their best life is the fear of what others will say and how they will respond. My prayer is that you would be delivered from the thoughts and opinions of others. Many have yet to move into the things that I have called them to because they are afraid of what everyone else is going to say and don't want to deal with possible condemnation from others. Thus, they go to the grave unfulfilled and full of potential because they were too afraid to step out on faith and believe that I love them for who they are. I know that this text is very controversial and will cause much discussion, which is why I am glad that it has been written. The world is full of hurting people. There are discussions that people do not know how to have and will refuse to have. This does not mean that it is right to leave people in the dark about issues that are real. People really do want to be different and most of all they want an authentic relationship with me, which is very attainable. In order to have this relationship with me, you must be true to yourself, others and me. Below is a prescription for being able to make it in life:

Love yourself: Flaws and All

The primary goal is for you to understand that there is a need to acknowledge the hurt of your life. Effectively communicate your hurt, express the new person that you would like to see, commit to lasting positive change and know you can have a better relationship with others and me. With the guidance of the Holy Spirit and ability to walk in truth, life can be better.. As long as people are not true to themselves, they cannot help others to walk in truth. All that they seek to do will not be accomplished to its total fulfillment, due to the lack of truth found in the foundation of their being.

I want readers to understand that in life there are struggles. When you learn to be vulnerable with me, you can view yourself from a much better perspective. I also would like you to understand Romans 8:28, which states, "And we know all things work together for the good of them who love God; to them who are called according to his purpose."

Hurt stems from childhood trauma, which turns into adulthood drama. The damage that done during a person's life causes problems and a need for security as well as significance. When damaged areas area challenged, problems occur. If not treated or addressed, they can become out of control. The problem with most individuals who are angry and hurt is that they do not know how to receive truth or express their truth without the fear of judgment and/or rejection. When a person has been attacked for so long by others, they tend to become very defensive. This causes them to live in denial. There is always a cycle to hurt if someone does not take the initiative to put it to an end.

The Bible is one the tool in which freedom can take place if interpreted correctly. It provides a foundation for psychological models and can help one view themselves from my perspective. There are many examples in the Bible about my power, amongst many other things. If you take heed by applying biblical principles as well as some secular principles, you can live a balanced life. The purpose of being able to integrate spirituality and life experiences causes maturity. It will also help you enter into a richer experience of worship and a more effective life of service.

You must assume responsibility for what has happened to you. The past cannot be changed, but your present can be with positive thinking and consistent behavior. This will help you to live in truth. The main factor to live in truth is being able to surrender to my agape love for you. When a person understands that they are loved by me, and actually loved by others despite their flaws, it causes them to know that they can also learn to love themselves.

When a person has acknowledged their truth and surrendered to the fact that I love them no matter what, this will allow room for change, growth and healthy development.

If a safe, judgment free zone were provided with love, empathy and compassion, there would be a stronger deliverance in the earth. When people are able to identify with the truth and the truth is encouraged, it will help them live in a place of liberty, being that lies only hold a person in different stages of bondage.

My desire is for you to be free. My hope is that if you have been in bondage, that this book has made you free or will provoke your spirit to find freedom. Do not allow anyone or anything to keep you in bondage any longer. Know that people will always have an opinion, but you have to know that it is not your duty to please everyone. Where most people go wrong at is that they give power to the unauthorized voices and end up allowing their voices to control their lives. Many people have fallen because of what everyone else has said about what they should be doing instead of being receptive to what I have called you to do. There is a declaration that I would like for you to say as an affirmation:

I have the power within me to accomplish what I have been called to do
I denounce the unauthorized voices that I have allowed to control my life and I regain my strength to hear clearly from God.
I understand that the work that I have been called to do may not be popular, but it will be effective in a positive manner.
I will not give up and I will not continue to live in guilt or fear because I accept my truth

I know that even in my flaws, I am loved and I am great in the eyes of God

No longer will I sit around and be a victim, but today I chose to be a victor

I forgive those who have done me wrong,

I forgive myself for doing wrong to others

I ask God to forgive me daily for wrong doing knowing and unknowing

I know that God will lead me into all truth and that all things that I go through

Are really working out for my good.

I may not understand it all at this moment, but I know that I am stronger because of my trials.

My life is WORTH LIVING and my story will help to save someone else.

No shame, no fear, no indecisiveness, no arrogance, no pride

I am what God says I am and that is all that matters

Terrell spoke the following words to close his sermon and I echo them to you:

"Even though people counted you out, including yourself, it was I who counted you in. When you were down and out, friends and family left you all alone because of your issues. I said that you would be like a tree, planted by the rivers of water and shall not be moved. It does not matter what they have said. All that matters is what I have said and currently say about your life and its purpose. People do not have a heaven or hell to put you into unless you allow them to. Greater am I in you if you have a relationship with me than he that is in the world. Yes, the words of others hurt, but there is life after the hurt. After the pain, after the agony, after the frustration, after the betrayal, there is still life for you.

"I say unto you, 'Well done.' Know that just because others said you would not make it in life, I have said something different and that is all that matters. Even though they said you wouldn't make it, my voice is stronger than that of the naysayer. Be encouraged and

strengthened in me. For in my presence there is fullness of joy and my joy is your strength. Continue to do your good works that I have assigned you to do. People don't have to understand what I am doing. As long as you understand and you commune with me, that is all that matters. My say so is the first and the final.

"I love you! I have created you and I make no mistakes! You are not a mistake, but you are a jewel in my eyes and in my kingdom. You are great. Continue to be holy because I am holy. Continue to love me as I will always love you, my child. From now on, I want you to look at yourself the way that I see you because I am the only one that matters. People and their opinions change, but I remain the same yesterday, today and forevermore.

"Evangelize in love and continue to win souls for my kingdom. Your reward shall be great and know that I am with you always even until the ends of the Earth. Never allow anything or anyone to separate us again. I am here just for you. To meet all of your needs and to fill the voids of life that has left you feeling empty. Don't fall into the traps of societal norms, but be authentically you. I made each of you as an original. He said negative things and she said negative things. However, you must know that I HAVE SAID DIFFERENTLY.

"When this book was written, it was written with everyone in mind. While reading this, I am sure that you have seen pieces of yourself through Terrell's life. The fact of the matter is you cannot look at your issues as being the end. Many aspects of life are to be explored as new experiences calling your name. The fact is you must change the perspective on how you view your struggle. Yes, it might be very difficult and yes, it may seem unfair.

However, know there is always someone who has a situation that is worse than your own. Take the cards that life deals and play the best honest game that you can with what you have been provided. Once you learn that the opinions of everyone else do not govern your life, you will be able to walk in liberty, truth and authenticity. Never allow those who expect you to fail because of your struggles to control your destiny. Take back your life and know that I am there with you. I am waiting on you to take a leap of faith and turn your tragedy into a triumph.

"Church is great if you are under the right leadership-leadership that will love you and allow you to be active in what God has called you to do. However, you can have a great relationship with me without attending a brick and mortar building. Many have been banned from church because of their issues, which is wrong. The church should be the place of refuge, deliverance, restoration and healing. You can be healed today. I want you to understand that I am waiting for you and that I will be more than happy to use you. You may say one thing, but I have said something different. I love you more than life.."

Signed,

God

ABOUT
The Author

J . Wesley was born on September 12, 1989 in Newark, NJ. Before he was ever formed in his mother's womb, he had a strong calling on his life. The Lord's presence was evident in him at a very young age. Even though he tried to run for many years, he learned through trial and error that he was not going to be fulfilled as long as he continued to run from God. Through the test and trials of life, J. Wesley is a true example of resilience and servant leadership. Wesley overcomes each trial, tribulation, and tragedy with grace that allows him the opportunity to sow into others who will endure the same things that he has.

Wesley holds a B.A. in Sociology, M.Ed in Education, Certificate in Pastoral Counseling and is currently pursuing a M.Div from Emory University Candler School of Theology with the desire to pursue doctoral studies after the completion of this degree. He loves education and believes strongly that with knowledge comes much power and accountability. Not only is he an educator, he is also a artist, public speaker, spiritual coach, minister, higher education professional and social advocate. He understands that he renders his services in a spirit of excellent and achievement. He teaches on spirituality, life development, leadership, education and other topics which have proven to be a success in the lives of those which he has come in contact with. At his age, he has accomplished a lot and contributes his success to God, family, friends and supporters.

J. Wesley hopes that through his writing, nuggets of wisdom and interactions with others that people will become delivered, healed and set free. He wants people to understand that they can have a personal relationship with God in spite of what society says. "You Said One Thing.... But God Said Differently: Silencing the Unauthorized Voices & Living Your Authentic Life" was written with each of you in mind. J. Wesley is not your typical person, but he believes strongly in practicing what he preaches with an emphasis on living in truth. He believes that people should accept and live their truth in order to experience true healing and deliverance. He lives by the mantra "If I can help somebody as I pass along, than my living will not be in vain".

Teach me your way, O Lord, that I may walk in your truth; unite my heart to fear your name. - Psalm 86:11

For more information, visit the website at www.jwesley.org

www.ingramcontent.com/pod-product-compliance
Lightning Source LLC
LaVergne TN
LVHW011332080426
835513LV00006B/312